The Aubergine Cookbook

The Aubergine Cookbook

Classic and contemporary recipes
for today's healthy diet

Rosemary Moon

APPLE

A QUINTET BOOK

Published by The Apple Press
6 Blundell Street
London N7 9BH

ISBN 1-85076-995-8

This book was designed and produced by
Quintet Publishing Limited
6 Blundell Street
London N7 9BH

Creative Director: Richard Dewing
Art Director: Silke Braun
Designer: Rita Wüthrich
Project Editor: Diana Steedman
Editor: Alexa Stace
Photographer: Iain Bagwell
Food Stylist: Lucy Miller

Typeset in Great Britain by
Central Southern Typesetters, Eastbourne
Manufactured in Singapore by Pica Colour Separation Overseas Pte Ltd.
Printed in Singapore by Star Standard Industries Pte Ltd.

Contents

Introduction

Above *The exquisite, white Ova variety clearly suggests why the aubergine is sometimes known as eggplant.*

Right *Slim Jim – an excellent aubergine for slicing.*

The aubergine is one of the most popular Mediterranean vegetables, and there is an increasing number of culinary enthusiasts, eager to experiment with this delicious vegetable.

Rounded and smooth, the most common varieties of aubergines range in colour from deep purple to pink, and often weigh upward of one pound/450 grammes. Roasted, baked or fried, they are the main ingredient in countless dishes, but can also be used as an extra, to turn an ordinary dish into something special. Aubergines marinate well, absorbing the flavours of seasoning and spices. It is not true that all aubergine dishes contain vast amounts of oil and must therefore be greasy. Many dishes can be almost fat-free if the aubergine is broiled or barbecued in preference to being fried. I still remember the delight and pleasure when I first tasted a grilled aubergine. The flesh assumes a glorious smokiness, a subtle flavour that can be savoured on its own, or used as a delicious background for dips and sauces. This flavour is even more pronounced when the aubergine is cooked over the barbecue, preferably over wood chips.

Aubergines Worldwide

Many cuisines around the world feature aubergines but it is Chinese, Greek, Turkish, Italian, Indian and Thai dishes that are especially associated with them and are a mainstay in their cooking.

China

Chinese dishes often include braised aubergines, and they are especially used by the numerous Buddhists who follow a strict vegetarian diet. Most Lo-han recipes in particular, which originated in the monasteries of China and Tibet, usually include aubergines.

Japan

In Japan the aubergine features largely in tempura, a delicate dish of fish and vegetable pieces dipped in a light batter and deep-fried until crisp and golden. In order to cook the aubergines as quickly as the other ingredients, the long, thin varieties are preferred over the round ones.

Above Ping Tung Long is popular in Asian cooking.
Below A selection of aubergines grown under glass.

Thai

Thai cooking often features aubergines, mostly using the long, thin, green varieties. These shapes are ideal for slicing or cutting into dice for salads. Another popular Thai variety is the pea aubergine, shaped as the name suggests and which are added to dishes whole. Pea aubergines look very attractive, but are often hard to find, except in specialist shops.

Italy

Rustic Italian cooking is full of aubergines, and many of the most famous dishes, such as Caponata (see page 40), are from Calabria in the south, known for robust and gutsy flavours. Long thin varieties are available in Italy as well as the more rounded ones, and they are interchangable in recipes, the shape being often of more importance for appearance rather than flavour.

India

Aubergines are used in the many different styles of Indian cooking, vegetarian and non-vegetarian. They are used extensively in main dishes, as well as in a wide variety of relishes and preserves. The ability of the aubergine to absorb flavours makes it a valuable ingredient in curries, and the appearance of dishes is often enhanced by adding chilli and turmeric.

Above Short Tom, a small, dark-purple vegetable, suitable for a wide variety of dishes.

Turkey

For many aubergine lovers it is not until the delights of Turkish cooking are explored that the true glory of the vegetable is revealed. Without the aubergine, it would seem, there is no Turkish cuisine. Turkish dishes are full of the mystery of smoky aubergine flesh, blended with tomatoes and oils, and an inspired blend of spices. The Turkish style is a wonderful mixture of warm Mediterranean flavours, married with the spiciness of north Africa and the Middle East.

The History of the Aubergine

Both India and China claim to be the original home of the aubergine, although there are no records of it growing in the wild. However, it is most likely that China was the source, and there are references to eggplants in records of market gardening dating from 500 BC.

It was certainly popular throughout Asia long before it reached Europe in the Middle Ages. Like so many "new" foods it was regarded at first with suspicion in the West, and was even referred to as the *apple of Sodom*! It was also regarded at first as a decorative plant, rather than one to eat and enjoy. In fact, it took a long time for the aubergine to be accepted in the West.

Varieties

Above The unusual Asian Bride variety is ideal for slicing..

Aubergines belong to the same family as potatoes, as do tomatoes and peppers. This is the deadly nightshade family, which might explain why aubergines had a bad press at first. All members of this family contain a certain amount of toxins, and in aubergines they are present in the immature fruits, in the stems and leaves. It is interesting to note that fruits picked when they are unripe do not keep for longer than a few hours at peak condition.

Many aubergines grow to over one pound/450 grammes in weight. These are regarded as large aubergines for the recipes, while a medium aubergine weighs about 12 ounces/350 grammes. Tiny finger aubergines, and the white egg-shaped ones, are excellent for relishes and preserves which require whole fruits. Thai aubergines – the long, thin variety – are best for Eastern-style cooking, especially if they are to be sliced and stir-fried with other vegetables.

I have geared this book mainly to the supermarket shopper, and the recipes therefore can all be made with the more common purple varieties. However, supermarkets are waking up to aubergine culture, and many are now stocking round fruits for stuffing, stripy ones for presentation, and the longer thin varieties which work well for Eastern cooking.

Salting

I am often asked whether it is necessary to salt aubergines before cooking, a technique used to extract any bitter juices from the flesh. In most cases it isn't, but I do salt aubergine slices to soften them for making a mould, or for a shell that is to be stuffed and baked. Salting is not necessary for frying or grilling, when I can safely say, having tried both ways, that it seems to make no difference at all to the outcome.

Above Turkish Orange aubergines are unusually juicy.

Left Bambino are about the size of cherries and may be boiled or roasted whole. They make wonderful additions to salads.

Buying and Storing

It is essential to buy aubergines when they are really fresh, with a dark, shiny and blemish-free skin. With most varieties the darker the skin the better. In addition to sweetness of flavour, a fresh aubergine will have a much more tender skin. You should also check that the stem is fresh-looking, and not shrivelled or bruised. Buy them as needed, but if you have to store them, they are best loosely wrapped in a plastic bag and kept in the salad drawer of the refrigerator.

Growing Aubergines

Aubergines make wonderful greenhouse plants, and I have grown them successfully without heat, although they do like humidity. Pinch out the tops when they reach two feet/60 centimetres tall, to encourage them to bush, and use canes as support, especially when the fruits appear.

They appear to need high temperatures to set, especially the more unusual varieties. Once the fruits have set and the flowers have faded, make sure that the flowers drop off, otherwise the fruits will be blemished. Feed generously once a week with a tomato fertilizer once the fruits have set. To encourage maximum growth, limit the number of fruits on each plant to between six and eight.

Above Display aubergines growing in a pit house at West Dean Gardens.

Natural Cooking Partners

As the aubergine absorbs other flavours so easily, there are some ingredients which are natural partners and will always produce a successful dish.

Tomatoes can be used in all forms, including passata, sun-dried tomatoes and tomato paste. The colour greatly enhances the appearance of aubergine dishes, while well-reduced tomato sauces also add richness.

Left Many varieties of aubergine make very attractive plants. This is the striped Rossa Bianca.

Below Japanese Pickling is a variety ideal for use in relishes and preserves.

Olive oils may be rich, green and fruity, or fragrant and light. Many dishes begin by frying aubergines in oil, so always use a well-flavoured, preferably extra virgin oil.

Meats with a certain amount of fat will not only flavour the dish, but also help to keep the aubergine moist. Stuffed aubergines are always successful when filled with a ground meat filling, such as pork, lamb or beef, as the fat content in the meat will help to soften the shells. However, for poultry or vegetable fillings with less fat, it is necessary to add stock or water to the baking dish, to enable the shells to cook through.

introduction

13

Above *The flowers of the aubergine range through pink and purple, and clearly show their close relationship to the potato.*

Aubergine Humus

Aubergine and Cheese Pâté

Aubergine Pesto

Aubergine, Fennel, and Walnut Salad

Aubergine and Orange Cream

Aubergine Toasts

Minted Aubergine Salad with Yogurt

Thai Salad

Cracked Wheat Salad

Aubergine Guacamole

Smoky Aubergine and Mint Dip

Ratatouille Niçoise

Aubergine à la Grecque

Aubergine Salad with Cranberries

Aubergine with Ginger

Aubergine and Lentil Salad

Aubergine and Shrimp Fritters

Crispy Aubergine Slices

Aubergine Cream

Aubergine Caviar

Aubergine with Tomatoes and Mozzarella

Aubergine Sandwiches

Spiced Aubergine Salad

Spring Rolls

Caponata

Barbecued Aubergine with Spicy Pepper Butter

Italian Grilled Aubergine

Grilled Aubergine and Goat's Cheese Salad

Aubergine Humus

For all humus fans. This version uses aubergine in place of chickpeas, but the tahini gives the dip the flavour that you would expect.

SERVES 6

- 1 large aubergine
- 3 spring onions, roughly chopped
- 1 red chilli, seeded and chopped
- Grated zest and juice of ½ lemon
- 2 garlic cloves, crushed
- Salt and freshly ground black pepper
- 3 Tbsp olive oil, plus extra for drizzling
- 100 ml/3½ fl oz tahini
- Paprika, to sprinkle

Preparation time: 30 minutes

❶ Cook the aubergine on a barbecue, under a grill or in a hot oven until the skin is wrinkled and blistered and the flesh is tender. Turn once or twice during cooking. Cover with a damp cloth and leave to cool for about 10 minutes, then peel off the skin.

❷ Roughly chop the aubergine, then mix it in a bowl with the remaining ingredients. Spoon the mixture into a small serving dish. Drizzle with a little extra olive oil and sprinkle with paprika. Serve with warmed pitta bread, or vegetable sticks for dipping.

Aubergine and Cheese Pâté

A creamy pâté to serve with toast or crackers. Use double cream or cottage cheese according to your conscience.

SERVES 6

- 1 large or 2 small aubergines
- 200 g/7 oz cream cheese
- 1 garlic clove, crushed
- 1 green chilli, seeded and chopped
- 1 Tbsp tomato paste
- Salt and freshly ground black pepper
- Paprika, to sprinkle

Preparation time: 40 minutes

Chilling time 30 minutes

❶ Cook the aubergine over a barbecue, under a grill or in a hot oven until the skin is wrinkled and blistered and the flesh is tender. Turn once or twice during cooking. Cover with a damp cloth and leave to cool for about 10 minutes, then peel off the skin.

❷ Blend the aubergine with the remaining ingredients in a blender. Season well, then turn into a serving bowl. Sprinkle with paprika. Chill for 30 minutes before serving.

Aubergine Pesto

A relatively low-in-fat pesto with a hint of smokiness from the aubergine. If fresh basil is unavailable, try mixing one teaspoon of dried basil into chopped fresh parsley instead.

SERVES 4

- 1 large aubergine
- 1 large handful of fresh basil leaves
- 2–3 garlic cloves, roughly chopped
- 50 g/1¾ oz pine nuts
- 50 g/1¾ oz freshly grated Parmesan cheese
- 1 tsp coarse sea salt
- 50 ml/2 fl oz olive oil
- Freshly cooked pasta, to serve
- Parmesan shavings and basil sprigs, to garnish

Preparation time: 40 minutes

❶ Cook the aubergine over a barbecue, under a grill or in a hot oven until the skin is wrinkled and blistered and the flesh is tender. Turn once or twice during cooking. Cover with a damp cloth and leave to cool slightly for about 10 minutes, then peel off the skin.

❷ Blend all the remaining ingredients together in a blender or food processor, then add the aubergine and blend again. Season to taste. Serve tossed with freshly cooked pasta.

appetizers and salads

17

Aubergine, Fennel and Walnut Salad

The slightly aniseed flavour of the fennel and the crunch of the nuts contrast well with the aubergine.

SERVES 6

- 175 ml/6 fl oz olive oil
- 1 fennel bulb, thinly sliced, feathery leaves reserved for garnish
- 1 small red onion, sliced
- 75 g/2¾ oz walnut pieces
- Sea salt and freshly ground black pepper
- 1 large aubergine, cut into ½-inch/1-cm pieces
- 1 Tbsp red wine vinegar
- 1 tomato, skinned, seeded and chopped
- 1 Tbsp torn fresh basil leaves
- Basil sprigs, to garnish

Preparation time: 15 minutes

Cooking time: 15 minutes

Cooling time: 30 minutes

---

❶ Heat 3 tablespoons of olive oil in a pan and add the fennel and onion. Cook until just soft but not browned, about 5 to 8 minutes. Remove with a slotted spoon and place in a salad bowl.

❷ Add 2 tablespoons of oil to the pan, then stir in the walnut pieces and fry them for about 2 minutes, until crisp and browned but not burnt. Remove the nuts from the pan with a slotted spoon and drain on paper towels. Place the nuts in a bowl, sprinkle with salt, and toss until well coated and cool.

❸ Add 4 tablespoons of oil to the pan, then add the aubergine and fry over a moderate heat until tender and browned on all sides. Remove from the pan and add to the fennel and onion.

❹ Add the remaining oil to the pan with the red wine vinegar and a little salt and pepper. Heat, stirring, until the dressing is simmering, then pour over the vegetables in the bowl. Toss lightly, then leave to cool for 10 to 15 minutes.

❺ When the salad is still just slightly warm, add the salted walnuts, chopped tomato and basil. Leave until cold, then serve garnished with fennel leaves and basil sprigs.

appetizers and salads

Aubergine and Orange Cream

An unusual cream with a Spanish flavour, using a fragrant olive oil, sage and orange. It is excellent served with roast or smoked duck.

SERVES 4 TO 6

- 2 aubergines
- Grated zest and juice of 1 large orange
- 1 garlic clove, crushed
- 1 Tbsp chopped fresh sage
- Salt and freshly ground black pepper
- 50 ml/2 fl oz fragrant Spanish olive oil

Preparation time: 30 minutes

❶ Cook the aubergines over a barbecue, under a grill or in a hot oven until the skin is wrinkled and blistered and the flesh is tender. Turn once or twice while cooking. Cover with a damp cloth and leave for about 10 minutes to cool.

❷ Peel the aubergines, then chop the flesh roughly. Place in a blender or liquidizer with all the remaining ingredients and blend to a thick paste, seasoning well with salt and pepper.

❸ Serve as a dip, with vegetables or olive bread, or as a sauce with duckling, either hot or cold.

Aubergine Toasts

This is a variation on the ever-popular Chinese prawn toasts. The aubergine can be shredded with a coarse grater, but you will find it easier to use a food processor.

SERVES 4

- 4 slices white bread, crusts removed
- Vegetable oil, for deep-frying
- Thinly sliced chillies and cilantro sprigs, to garnish
- Oyster sauce, to serve

EGGPLANT PASTE:

- 225 g/½ lb aubergine, peeled and shredded
- 1 egg white, lightly whisked
- 2 tsp sherry
- 2 tsp oyster sauce
- Pinch of ground ginger
- 2 tsp cornflour
- Pinch of salt

Preparation time: 20 minutes
Cooking time: 10 minutes

❶ Mix the aubergine with the remaining paste ingredients. Cut the bread into bite-sized triangles, then spread on one side with the paste.

❷ Heat the oil to 160°C/320°F in a wok, then carefully add the triangles in batches with a spoon, paste side down, and fry for about 2 to 3 minutes, until the bread is golden brown. Remove with a slotted spoon and drain on paper towels. Keep warm until all the toasts are cooked.

❸ Serve warm with oyster sauce, garnished with sliced chillies and cilantro sprigs.

Aubergine Toasts

Minted Aubergine Salad with Yogurt

A creamy salad to serve with cold roast meat or poached salmon. I like to spice it up a bit with toasted cumin seeds, but fennel or coriander seeds work just as well.

SERVES 4 TO 6

- 1 Tbsp cumin seeds
- 100 ml/3½ fl oz fruity olive oil
- 1 large aubergine, sliced
- 1 garlic clove, crushed
- 2 Tbsp chopped fresh mint
- 225 ml/8 fl oz natural yogurt
- Salt and freshly ground black pepper

Preparation time: 35 minutes

Cooling time: about 45 minutes

---

❶ Heat a large pan over a moderate heat, then add the cumin seeds and dry-fry for 30 seconds or so, until fragrant and just starting to pop. Transfer to a saucer and leave until required.

❷ Heat the oil in the pan, then add the aubergine slices and fry on both sides until lightly browned and tender. Do not be tempted to add more oil as some will run from the aubergine as it cooks. Remove the slices from the pan with a slotted spoon and allow to cool a little, then place them in a shallow dish, sprinkle with the cumin, garlic and mint and leave until cold.

❸ Spoon on the yogurt and season well, then toss together gently. Serve lightly chilled.

appetizers and salads

22

Thai Salad

Bright with the flavours of the Pacific, this is an exciting main course salad. Use ham in place of pork if you prefer, and mint instead of cilantro for a change.

SERVES 4

- 2 long, thin Thai or Japanese-style aubergines
- 2 hot Thai chillies, seeded if preferred, and finely sliced
- 2 shallots, finely sliced
- 2 Tbsp fish sauce
- Juice of two limes
- 1 Tbsp caster sugar
- 50 g/1¾ oz finely chopped cooked pork
- 125 g/4½ oz peeled prawns, defrosted if frozen
- 2 Tbsp fresh whole coriander leaves

Preparation time: 30 minutes

---

❶ Cook the aubergines over a barbecue, under a grill, or in a hot oven until the skin is wrinkled and blistered and the flesh is tender. Turn once or twice while cooking. Cover with a damp cloth and leave for about 10 minutes to cool. Meanwhile, mix together the chillies, shallots, fish sauce, lime juice and sugar in a bowl.

❷ Peel the aubergines and cut them into chunks. Toss the aubergines in the sauce, then add the pork and prawn. Serve garnished with the cilantro leaves.

Cracked Wheat Salad

I love cracked wheat salads. The addition of aubergine, with its lovely purple-black skin, provides lots of colour and texture.

SERVES 3 TO 4

- 200 g/7 oz cracked wheat
- Half a cucumber, finely diced
- 2 large tomatoes, seeded and chopped
- 100 ml/3½ fl oz olive oil
- 1 onion, finely sliced
- 1 aubergine, sliced, then slices halved
- 2 tsp ground cinnamon
- Salt and freshly ground black pepper
- 2 Tbsp raisins
- 1 Tbsp red wine vinegar
- 2 Tbsp chopped chives
- 2 tbsp chopped fresh parsley

Preparation time: 30 minutes

Cooking time: 15 minutes

❶ Place the cracked wheat in a bowl and just cover with cold water. Leave to stand for 20 to 30 minutes, until the wheat has absorbed all the water. Turn into a fine nylon sieve, and press out any surplus water with the back of a large spoon. Place in a large bowl and add the cucumber and tomato.

❷ Heat the oil in a pan and add the onion, aubergine and cinnamon. Cook until browned on all sides,

then remove from the pan with a slotted spoon. Season the cracked wheat well, then add the raisins.

❸ Add the vinegar to any oil remaining in the pan, season lightly then pour over the wheat. Add the chives and parsley and mix well. Arrange the onion and aubergine on top of the salad before serving.

TIP

Cracked wheat, available from good health food stores, is the lightly crushed grain of wheat. It is sometimes called bulghar wheat, and is a nutritious staple in the Middle East. Delicious in salads and it also makes excellent pilaf – see Aubergine and Cracked Wheat Pilaf on page 95.

Aubergine Guacamole

For all diet-conscious lovers of Mexican food! This is a lower-calorie version of the traditional avocado dip.

SERVES 4 TO 6

- 1 large aubergine
- 1 avocado, peeled and finely chopped
- Grated zest and juice of 1 lime
- 2 tomatoes, seeded and chopped
- 1 green chilli, seeded and finely chopped
- 1 Tbsp very finely chopped onion
- 1–2 garlic cloves, crushed
- Salt and freshly ground black pepper
- Olive oil, to drizzle
- Paprika, to sprinkle

Preparation time: 10 minutes
Cooking time: 40 minutes

❶ Preheat the oven to 220°C/425°F/ Gas Mark 7. Prick the aubergine all over, then place on a baking sheet and roast for 30 to 40 minutes, until the skin is wrinkled and blistered, and the flesh is tender. Turn once or twice during cooking. Cover with a damp cloth and leave to cool completely.

❷ Peel the aubergine, then chop into small pieces. Blend to a fairly smooth paste in a blender or food processor, then turn into a small bowl. Toss the avocado in the lime juice, then add to the aubergine with the remaining ingredients. Stir carefully until well combined. Season generously with salt and pepper, then drizzle with a little olive oil and sprinkle with paprika.

❸ Serve in a small bowl with tortilla chips or warm toast.

Smoky Aubergine and Mint Dip

A refreshing salad to serve as a dip, or on a bed of salad leaves.

SERVES 4

- 2 large aubergines
- 2 tsp cumin seeds
- 1–2 garlic cloves, roughly chopped
- 2 Tbsp chopped fresh mint leaves
- Sea salt and freshly ground black pepper
- 225 ml/8 fl oz thick natural yogurt
- 1 cucumber, finely diced

Preparation time: 10 minutes
Cooking time: about 30 minutes

❶ Cook the aubergines over a barbecue, under a grill, or in a hot oven until until the skin is wrinkled and blistered and the flesh is tender. Turn once or twice during cooking. Cover with a damp cloth and leave to cool for about 10 minutes, then peel off the skin.

❷ While the aubergines are grilling, toast the cumin seeds in a dry pan until just starting to pop, then transfer them to a mortar and allow

to cool for a few minutes. Add the garlic, mint, and about ½ teaspoon of salt, then grind into a paste. Alternatively, crush with the end of a rolling pin.

❸ Chop the aubergine. Place in a blender with the cumin paste and blend into a thick purée. Add the yogurt and blend to a creamy paste. Turn into a bowl, stir in the cucumber and season to taste with salt and pepper.

Aubergine Guacamole

Ratatouille Niçoise

This is more a salad than a vegetable stew, with the ingredients cooked individually, but it has all the flavours of the classic Mediterranean dish.

SERVES 4 AS A MAIN COURSE, OR 8 AS AN APPETIZER

- About 6 Tbsp olive oil
- 1 large onion, chopped
- 2 garlic cloves, finely sliced
- 1 green pepper, cored, seeded and sliced
- 1 courgette, yellow if possible, sliced
- 1 long, thin aubergine, cut into 6-mm/¼-inch slices
- 400 g/14 oz tinned chopped tomatoes
- 150 ml/5 fl oz red wine
- 4–5 sprigs fresh thyme
- Salt and freshly ground black pepper
- 1 Tbsp torn fresh basil leaves
- 75 g/2¾ oz small black stoned olives
- 200 g/7 oz diced feta cheese

Preparation time: 10 minutes
Cooking time: 30 minutes
Cooling time: 20–30 minutes

---

❶ Heat 3 tablespoons of olive oil in a large pan, add the onion and cook over a medium heat until softened but not brown, about 5 minutes. Add the garlic and cook for a few seconds longer, then remove the onion and garlic with a slotted spoon and place in a large bowl.

❷ Add the green pepper to the pan and cook slowly for 4 to 5 minutes, then remove with a slotted spoon and place in the bowl. Add 1 to 2 tablespoons more oil to the pan, then add the courgette and cook for 3 to 4 minutes, turning once.

❸ Remove the courgette with a slotted spoon and add to the bowl. Add 1 to 2 more tablespoons of oil to the pan, then add the aubergine slices and fry gently until lightly browned on both sides. It may be necessary to do this in batches. Remove the aubergine with a slotted spoon and add to the bowl.

❹ Add the tomatoes to the pan with the red wine, thyme, salt and pepper. Bring to the boil, then simmer gently for 5 minutes. Remove the thyme, then pour the hot sauce over the vegetables in the bowl. Leave to cool, tossing the vegetables in the sauce once or twice.

❺ Just before serving, add the torn basil leaves, olives and cheese. Serve at room temperature for the best flavour.

Aubergine à la Grecque

A marinated aubergine salad with mushrooms and chopped parsley. Serve with lots of bread to mop up the delicious juices.

SERVES 4 TO 6

- 1 large aubergine, sliced
- About 100 ml/3½ fl oz olive oil
- Salt and freshly ground black pepper
- 1–2 garlic cloves, crushed
- 250 g/9 oz mushrooms, sliced
- 2–3 Tbsp chopped fresh parsley

Preparation time: 25 minutes

Chilling time: 1–2 hours

---

❶ Preheat the grill. Arrange the aubergine slices in the pan and brush with olive oil. Grill until browned, turning occasionally.

❷ Place the aubergine slices in a serving dish and add enough oil to moisten, but not so much that they are swimming in it. Season well, add the garlic, mushrooms and parsley and stir gently. Leave for 1 to 2 hours, then serve at room temperature for best flavour.

Aubergine Salad with Cranberries

I have used cranberries in this recipe, but you could just as well use pomegranate juice and seeds. The sweet tartness of the fruit complements the aubergine very well.

SERVES 4 TO 6

- 3 Tbsp mild, fragrant olive oil
- 1 aubergine, cut into 6-mm/¼-inch dice
- 1 small onion, finely sliced
- 100 ml/3½ fl oz cranberry juice
- 1 garlic clove, crushed
- 40 g/1½ oz dried cranberries
- Salt and freshly ground black pepper
- 7 Tbsp toasted wholewheat breadcrumbs
- Chopped fresh parsley, to garnish

Preparation time: 10 minutes

Cooking time: 15 minutes

Cooling time: 30 minutes

---

❶ Heat the oil in a frying pan, add the aubergine and onion and cook over a moderate heat until the oil has all been absorbed. Add the cranberry juice and continue cooking until the aubergine is soft. Transfer to a serving bowl, add the garlic and allow to cool.

❷ Add the dried cranberries and season to taste. Stir in the toasted breadcrumbs and sprinkle with parsley just before serving.

Aubergine with Ginger

An Oriental salad to serve with any Chinese, Japanese or Thai meal. The clean taste of ginger provides a perfect appetizer.

SERVES 4

- 2 large aubergines
- 5-cm/2-inch piece fresh ginger
- 2 Tbsp light soy sauce
- 2 Tbsp sesame oil
- 1 Tbsp torn fresh coriander leaves
- Salt and sugar, to taste

Preparation time: 30–40 minutes

Marinating time: 15 minutes

❶ Cook the aubergines on a barbecue, under a grill or in a hot oven until the skin is wrinkled and blistered and the flesh is tender. Turn once or twice during cooking. Cover with a damp cloth and leave to cool for about 10 minutes, then peel off the skin. Cut the flesh into large pieces and place in a bowl.

❷ Grate the ginger coarsely, including the skin, then gather up the shreds in your hand, and squeeze the juice over the warm aubergine. Add all the remaining ingredients, stir well and leave for 10 to 15 minutes to marinate. Serve on a bed of lightly stir-fried pepper strips, or other Oriental vegetables.

appetizers and salads

Aubergine and Lentil Salad

An excellent winter salad as an alternative to coleslaw – filling and tasty.

SERVES 4

- 3 Tbsp sesame seeds
- 5 Tbsp olive oil
- 1 large onion, finely chopped
- 1 tsp ground cumin
- 1–2 garlic cloves, crushed
- 1 large aubergine, diced
- 100 g/3⅓ oz yellow lentils
- 400 g/14 oz tinned chopped tomatoes
- 250 ml/9 fl oz vegetable or chicken stock
- Salt and freshly ground black pepper
- 1 Tbsp freshly chopped mint

Preparation time: 10 minutes
Cooking time: 35 minutes

❶ Heat a large pan over a medium heat, then add the sesame seeds and fry for 2 to 3 minutes, stirring constantly, until evenly toasted. Transfer onto a plate.

❷ Heat 3 tablespoons of the oil in the pan. Add the onion and cumin and cook until starting to brown, then add the garlic and aubergine and continue cooking for 2 to 3 minutes. Add the lentils, chopped tomatoes, stock and seasoning. Bring to the boil. Cover and simmer for 30 minutes. Season and leave to cool.

❸ Add the toasted sesame seeds and mint to the mixture, then stir in the remaining olive oil. Cool the salad for 30 minutes before serving. Do not serve too cold, or the full flavour will be lost.

Aubergine and Prawn Fritters

I usually steer clear of dishes which need to be deep-fried, but these Italian-style fritters are so delicious that they make an exception to my rule.

SERVES 4

- 1 large aubergine, thickly sliced
- 100 g/3½ oz peeled prawns, finely chopped
- Vegetable oil, for deep-frying

BATTER:

- 3 large eggs
- 75 g/2¾ oz freshly grated Parmesan
- Salt and freshly ground black pepper
- Freshly grated nutmeg
- 3 Tbsp plain flour
- 3 Tbsp white breadcrumbs
- Lemon slices, halved, to garnish

Preparation time: 20 minutes
Cooking time: 30 minutes

❶ Add the aubergine slices to a large pan of boiling water and boil for 5 minutes. Drain and when cool enough squeeze the slices dry and mix them with the chopped prawns.

❷ Separate 2 eggs, reserving the whites. Mix the yolks with the cheese, and season with salt, pepper and nutmeg, then mix with the aubergines and prawns.

❸ Shape into 12 walnut-sized balls. Add the remaining egg to the reserved egg whites and beat them together. Spread the flour and the breadcrumbs on 2 plates. Coat the balls in the flour, dip them into the egg and then into the crumbs.

❹ Heat the oil in a deep-fryer to 190°C/375°F. Fry the fritters in batches until they are golden brown and crisp. Drain on paper towels. Serve either hot or cold, garnished with lemon slices.

Aubergine and Prawn Fritters

Crispy Aubergine Slices

This is a good appetizer for an informal supper party as it can be prepared well in advance, and baked as your guests arrive.

SERVES 4

• Vegetable oil
• 2 large eggs, beaten
• 1 Tbsp milk
• 100 g/3½ oz wholewheat breadcrumbs
• 2 Tbsp chopped fresh parsley
• 25 g/1 oz grated Parmesan cheese
• 40 g/1½ oz pine nuts, finely ground
• 50 g/1¾ oz cornmeal or polenta
• Salt and freshly ground black pepper
• 1 aubergine, cut into 1-cm/½-inch slices
• Salad leaves, to garnish

Preparation time: 20 minutes

Cooking time: 30 minutes

❶ Preheat the oven to 180°C/350°F/Gas Mark 4 and oil 2 baking sheets. Beat the eggs and milk together in a shallow bowl. Mix all the other ingredients except the aubergine on a flat plate.

❷ Dip the aubergine slices first into the egg, then into the crumb mix, coating them thoroughly. Place in a single layer on the baking sheets. Bake in the preheated oven for 30 minutes, or until the aubergine slices are tender and the crumbs are crisp. Serve garnished with salad leaves.

Aubergine Cream

Sometimes called Hünkâr Begendi *or* Sultan's Delight, *this delicate creamy dish is served as a sauce for meat or fish, or as a dip with pitta bread.*

SERVES 6 TO 8

• 2 large aubergines
• 1 Tbsp lemon juice
• 50 g/2 oz butter
• 4 Tbsp plain flour
• 450 ml/16 fl oz milk
• Salt and freshly ground black pepper
• 50 g/1¾ oz freshly grated Parmesan
• Chopped fresh parsley, to garnish
• Pitta bread, to serve

Preparation time: 20–40 minutes

Cooking time: 30 minutes

❶ Cook the aubergines under the grill or in a hot oven until the skins are wrinkled and blistered and the flesh is tender, turning once or twice. Cover with a damp cloth and leave to stand for about 10 minutes, then peel off the skin. Leave the aubergine flesh in a bowl of cold water with the lemon juice to prevent discoloration.

❷ Melt the butter in a large pan, then remove from the heat and stir in the flour. Cook slowly over a low heat for about 2 minutes, then put the pan to one side. Drain the aubergine and squeeze dry with your hands. Add to the pan and blend with a potato masher. Gradually stir in the milk.

❸ Bring the sauce slowly to the boil over a low heat, then season to taste. Simmer the sauce for about 15 minutes. Stir in the cheese, then season again if necessary. Pour into a warm bowl or dish and sprinkle with chopped parsley.

appetizers and salads

Aubergine Cream

Aubergine Caviar

Aubergine pastes have long been referred to as caviar. Nothing like the real thing, but the texture is slightly similar – a rough purée with a savoury tang.

SERVES 4

- 2 aubergines
- Salt and freshly ground black pepper
- Walnut oil
- 2 large tomatoes, chopped
- 1 large garlic clove, chopped
- 6 spring onions, chopped
- 1 Tbsp fresh chopped oregano
- 2 hard-boiled eggs, chopped very fine

Preparation time: 1 hour

Chilling time: 1 hour

❶ Preheat the oven to 220°C/425°F/ Gas Mark 7. Prick the aubergines all over, then place them on a baking sheet and season lightly. Drizzle with a little walnut oil, then bake in the preheated oven for 30 to 40 minutes, or until tender. Leave to cool, then roughly chop the aubergines, including the skin.

❷ Purée the aubergines in a food processor with the tomatoes, garlic and spring onions and enough walnut oil to make a paste. Season well, then stir in the oregano and chopped eggs. Chill slightly, then serve with fresh hot toast.

Aubergine with Tomatoes and Mozzarella

A simple dish to serve as a main course salad or an appetizer, with crusty bread to mop up the juices.

SERVES 4

- 2 large aubergines, cut lengthwise into 6-mm/¼-inch slices
- Salt and freshly ground black pepper
- 5 Tbsp olive oil
- Small handful of fresh basil leaves, roughly torn
- 8 small ripe tomatoes, halved
- 2 garlic cloves, finely sliced
- 125 g/4½ oz mozzarella, drained and thinly sliced
- 1 tsp balsamic vinegar

Preparation time: 40 minutes

Cooking time: 30 minutes

❶ Make a single layer of the aubergine slices on a baking sheet and sprinkle generously with salt. Leave for at least 30 minutes, then rinse thoroughly under cold water and pat dry with paper towels.

❷ Pour the oil into a shallow dish. Dip each slice of aubergine into the oil, then cook the slices, a few at a time, in a ridged grill pan for 3 to 4 minutes on each side.

❸ Layer the aubergine in an ovenproof dish with the basil, tomatoes and garlic. Finish with a layer of aubergine, season well, then cover with the sliced mozzarella.

❹ Add the balsamic vinegar to the oil left in the pan and pour it over the cheese. Grill under a moderate heat for 4 to 5 minutes, until the cheese is bubbling and starting to brown. Serve with mixed salad leaves and bread to mop up the juices.

Aubergine Sandwiches

This recipe uses slices of aubergine as the "bread" in baked ham and cheese sandwiches. They are delicious.

SERVES 4

- 1 large aubergine, cut lengthways into eight 6-mm/¼-inch slices
- Salt
- Olive oil, for brushing
- 2 slices ham, smoked turkey, or cooked chicken
- 2 slices Cheddar or other sharp cheese
- 1 large egg, beaten
- 1 Tbsp milk
- 100 g/3½ oz fresh white breadcrumbs
- Salad leaves, to garnish

Preparation time: 20 minutes plus 30 minutes salting time

Cooking time: 20 minutes

---

❶ Lay the aubergine slices on a baking sheet in a single layer, then sprinkle salt over them and leave for 30 minutes. Rinse under cold water and pat dry on paper towels.

❷ Preheat the oven to 200°C/400°F/ Gas Mark 6. Brush the slices lightly with olive oil on the outsides, then assemble them into 4 sandwiches. Fill each one with half a slice of cheese and half a slice of ham, trimming them to fit so that the filling does not overflow.

❸ Dip the sandwiches into the egg, beaten with the milk, then into the breadcrumbs. Press on sufficient breadcrumbs to give a good coating.

❹ Place the sandwiches on an oiled baking sheet and bake in the preheated oven for 20 minutes, or until lightly browned. Serve immediately with a salad garnish.

appetizers and salads

37

Spiced Aubergine Salad

This is based on a traditional north African recipe, where the aubergine is flavoured with paprika, cumin and lemon juice.

SERVES 4 TO 6

- About 250 ml/9 fl oz olive oil
- 2 aubergines, sliced
- 2 tsp sweet paprika
- 2 tsp ground cumin
- 2 garlic cloves, finely sliced
- 75 g/2¾ oz pistachio kernels
- Grated zest and juice of 1 lemon
- Salt and freshly ground black pepper
- Sugar, to taste

Preparation time: 10 minutes

Cooking time: 15 minutes

❶ Heat half the oil in a large pan and add the aubergine, paprika and cumin. Cook over a gentle heat so that the spices do not burn, adding more oil as necessary; the aubergine will take about 10 minutes to cook through. Add the garlic to the pan halfway through the cooking.

❷ Transfer the aubergine to a serving bowl, then add the pistachios, lemon zest and juice. Season well, adding a little sugar if you wish. Allow the salad to chill for about an hour before serving.

Spring Rolls

A variation on the popular Chinese dish, delicious dipped in soy sauce.

SERVES 4

- 3 Tbsp groundnut oil, plus extra for brushing
- 1 aubergine, sliced
- 1 small onion, finely sliced
- 3 Tbsp oyster sauce
- 100 ml/3½ fl oz water
- 175 g/6 oz prepared stir-fry vegetables, defrosted if frozen
- Salt
- 8 sheets filo pastry, measuring about 17.5 x 30 cm/7 x 12 inches
- Soy sauce

Preparation time: 1 hour

Cooking time: 15 minutes

❶ Heat the oil in a pan, add the aubergine and onion and cook gently. Mix the oyster sauce with the water, add to the pan and continue to cook slowly for about 10 minutes, until the aubergine is tender. Remove from the heat and leave until cool enough to handle.

❷ Preheat the oven to 200°C/400°F/ Gas Mark 6 and lightly oil a baking sheet. Mix the aubergine and onion with the stir-fry vegetables. Fold the filo sheets in half and brush with oil to keep them moist. Divide the vegetable mixture between them. Sprinkle each one with a few drops of soy sauce.

❸ Fold the bottom and sides of the pastry in over the filling, then roll the pastry up into a sausage, brushing the edges with a little oil. Place on the prepared baking sheet and brush lightly with oil again.

❹ Bake the spring rolls in the preheated oven for 10 to 15 minutes, until the pastry is crisp.

appetizers and salads

Spring Rolls

Caponata

The region of Calabria in southern Italy is famed for the pungency of its dishes, with the exciting flavours of simple ingredients skilfully blended together. Caponata is one of the most famous of all aubergine dishes and there are many supposedly authentic recipes for it. This is my personal favourite.

SERVES 4

- 2 large aubergines, cut into1-cm/ ½-inch chunks
- Salt
- 100 ml/3½ fl oz fruity olive oil
- 250 g/9 oz mixed pickled vegetables, such as onions, gherkins, peppers, roughly chopped
- 3 Tbsp capers
- 2 celery sticks, chopped fine
- 50 g/1¾ oz stoned green olives
- 1 Tbsp sugar
- 150 ml/5 fl oz red wine vinegar
- 2 Tbsp pine nuts

Preparation time: 45 minutes

Cooking time: 30 minutes

---

❶ Layer the aubergines in a colander, sprinkling each layer with salt, then leave to stand for 30 minutes. Rinse thoroughly in cold water, then drain and pat dry on paper towels.

❷ Pour all but 2 tablespoons of the oil into a large pan, add the aubergine and cook for 10 to 12 minutes, or until browned and soft.

❸ Pour the remaining oil into a small pan, add the pickles, capers, celery and olives and cook slowly over a very low heat for about 10 minutes, until well softened. Add the sugar and vinegar and continue to cook slowly until the smell of the vinegar has gone.

❹ Drain the aubergines of any excess oil, then add to the other vegetables with the pine nuts. Add a little salt to season, if necessary. Serve the caponata warm or cold.

TIP

The best way to buy stoned green olives is loose at a good delicatessen. They keep well for a couple of weeks in the refrigerator. Aside from being available for your cooking, they make irresistible pre-dinner nibbles.

Barbecued Aubergine with Spicy Pepper Butter

An unusual appetizer to keep the folks happy while the meat is cooking on the barbecue. Serve with soft rolls or pitta bread.

SERVES 4

- 2 aubergines

SPICY BUTTER:

- 125 g/4½ oz butter
- 1 tsp finely chopped onion
- 1 garlic clove, crushed
- ½ tsp paprika
- ½ tsp green peppercorns, crushed
- 1 Tbsp chopped fresh coriander
- Salt and freshly ground black pepper

Preparation time: 10 minutes

Plus chilling time: 1 hour

Cooking time: 40 minutes

❶ To make the spicy butter, beat the butter in a bowl with a wooden spoon until soft, then add all the remaining seasonings with salt and pepper to taste. Shape the butter into a roll, then cover in plastic wrap and chill for 1 hour.

❷ Cook the aubergines on the barbecue until the skins are blistered and wrinkled, and the flesh is tender. Turn them over several times during cooking. Do not cook them too quickly or the skins will burst.

❸ Carefully remove the aubergines from the barbecue, then cut them in half lengthwise. Score the soft flesh into diamonds, then top with a generous knob of the spicy butter and allow it to melt into the flesh.

Italian Grilled Aubergine

An Italian-style salad of cooked aubergine slices marinated in oil and mint and finished with toasted pine nuts and Parmesan.

SERVES 4

- 1 large aubergine, thickly sliced
- Olive oil, for brushing
- 40 g/1½ oz pine nuts, toasted
- 2 Tbsp chopped fresh parsley
- Grated zest of 1 lemon
- Parmesan cheese shavings

MARINADE:

- 100 ml/3½ fl oz olive oil
- 1 garlic clove, crushed
- 12 large basil leaves, roughly torn
- 1 Tbsp chopped fresh mint
- Salt and freshly ground black pepper
- 1 Tbsp balsamic vinegar

Preparation time: 20–25 minutes

Standing time: 1–2 hours

❶ Preheat the grill until very hot, then add the aubergine slices. Brush generously with olive oil, then grill until browned, turning frequently.

❷ Mix together the ingredients for the marinade in a shallow dish. Add the aubergine slices and turn them in the mixture. Leave for 1 to 2 hours, then stir in the pine nuts. Serve at room temperature, sprinkled with the parsley, lemon rind and Parmesan.

Italian Grilled Aubergine

Grilled Aubergine and Goat's Cheese Salad

In this marinated salad the spiced aubergine slices are grilled and served hot with goat's cheese. Do try a true goat's cheese, it is so good. The real thing should be eaten at its freshest.

SERVES 4

- 1 aubergine, thinly sliced
- Olive oil, for frying
- 100 g/3½ oz ripened goat's cheese, sliced

MARINADE:

- 1½ tsp cumin seeds
- ½ tsp coarse sea salt
- 100 ml/3½ fl oz red wine
- 2 Tbsp olive oil
- 1 Tbsp red wine vinegar
- Salt and freshly ground black pepper
- 1 garlic clove, crushed
- 1 Tbsp chopped fresh mint
- 1 tsp sugar

Preparation time: 45 minutes

Cooking time: 20 minutes

❶ To make the marinade, heat a small frying pan, then add the cumin seeds and fry them for 30 to 45 seconds, until fragrant and starting to brown. Turn the seeds into a mortar with the sea salt and pound them with a pestle until finely ground. Alternatively, crush with the end of a rolling pin.

❷ Transfer the spice mixture to a shallow dish and add the remaining marinade ingredients. Add the aubergine slices, turning to coat well, then leave for at least 30 minutes.

❸ Shake the aubergine slices dry, and reserve the marinade. Grill the slices with a little oil in a grill pan. Place in an ovenproof dish and top with the sliced cheese.

❹ Drizzle with the remaining marinade then grill under moderate heat until lightly browned. Serve with crusty bread and a juicy, tomato salad.

Red Mullet with Aubergine and Lovage Pesto

Crab-topped Aubergine Slices

Prawn and Aubergine Pasties

Aubergine and Tuna Risotto

Tuna and Aubergine Kebabs

Aubergine with Gingered Crab and Vanilla Pasta

Roast Monkfish with Aubergine and Wine Sauce

Aubergine and Cod Bake

Stuffed Trout with Pine Nuts

Trout with Aubergine and Cranberry Sauce

Braised Squid with Aubergine

Marinated Swordfish with Aubergine Ribbons

Stuffed Mussels

Deep-fried Fish with Aubergine Couscous

Almond-coated Fishcakes with Thai Salad

Mediterranean Fish Stew

Salmon and Aubergine Kedgeree

Skate with Blackened Aubergine Butter

Fish and Aubergine Pie

Fish Dishes

Red Mullet with Aubergine and Lovage Pesto

A light fish dish with very robust flavours. Red mullet has a meaty taste which balances the pesto very well.

Preparation time: 45 minutes

Cooking time: 20 minutes

❶ First prepare the pesto. Place all the ingredients in a blender or food processor and blend to a smooth sauce. Season to taste, then turn into a small bowl.

❷ Lay the aubergine slices in a single layer on a baking sheet. Sprinkle with salt and leave for 30 minutes. Preheat the oven to 200°C/400°F/Gas Mark 6. Rinse the aubergine well under cold water and dry on paper towels. Heat the oil in a pan, add the aubergines and cook until browned on both sides. Remove and keep warm in the oven.

❸ Add more oil to the pan if necessary. Add the mullet fillets, skin side down, and cook for 1 to 2 minutes. Transfer the fish to a buttered baking sheet and cook in the oven for 5 to 6 minutes.

❹ To serve, arrange 2 aubergine slices on individual warmed serving plates, then place a mullet fillet on each. Spoon a little of the pesto onto the plates, then serve immediately.

SERVES 4

- 2 aubergines, cut lengthways into 1-cm/½-inch slices
- Salt
- 2–3 Tbsp olive oil
- 8 large red mullet fillets
- Butter, for greasing

PESTO:

- 1 cup mixed lovage and parsley leaves, about half and half
- 50 g/1¾ oz freshly grated Parmesan cheese
- 40 g/1½ oz pine nuts
- 2 garlic cloves, crushed
- 100 ml/3½ fl oz olive oil
- Salt and freshly ground black pepper

Crab-topped Aubergine Slices

Crab and aubergine have very complementary flavours. A little crab meat goes a long way in this dish, so it's not expensive to make.

SERVES 4 AS AN APPETIZER,

2 AS A MAIN COURSE

- 1 aubergine, sliced lengthwise into 4
- Salt
- Olive oil, for frying
- 50 g/1¾ oz fresh white breadcrumbs
- 25 g/1 oz pine nuts
- Salt and freshly ground black pepper
- 50 g/1¾ oz freshly grated Parmesan cheese
- 1 Tbsp chopped fresh parsley
- 1–2 Tbsp melted butter
- 125 g/4½ oz crab meat

Preparation time: 50 minutes

Cooking time: 15 minutes

❶ Sprinkle the aubergine slices lightly with salt, then leave them to drain in a colander for 30 minutes. Preheat the oven to 220°C/425°F/ Gas Mark 7.

❷ Rinse the aubergine thoroughly in cold water, then dry on paper towels. Heat 2 tablespoons of oil in a pan and cook the slices for 3 to 4 minutes on each side, until just cooked. Transfer the aubergine to a baking sheet.

❸ Mix all the remaining ingredients together, binding them with the melted butter. Spoon onto the aubergine slices, then bake in the hot oven for 15 minutes, until the crab topping is lightly browned. Serve immediately, garnished with fresh parsley.

Prawn and Aubergine Turnovers

These delicious light turnovers make an ideal quick lunch, served with a salad.

SERVES 4

- Butter, for greasing
- 1 aubergine, cut into small pieces
- 1 red and 1 green pepper, cored, seeded and cut into small pieces
- 1 red onion, finely chopped
- 3–4 Tbsp mild, fragrant olive oil
- 400 g/14 oz cooked peeled prawns
- 175 g/6 oz cooked diced potato
- 3 Tbsp freshly chopped parsley
- Salt and freshly ground black pepper
- Grated zest and juice of ½ lemon
- 375 g/13 oz prepared puff pastry
- Milk, for glazing

Preparation time: 15 minutes

Cooking time: 25 minutes

❶ Preheat the oven to 200°C/400°F/ Gas Mark 6 and lightly butter a baking sheet.

❷ Heat the oil in a pan. Add the aubergine, peppers and onion and cook until just softened, then mix with the prawns, potato and parsley. Season the mixture and mix in the lemon zest and juice.

❸ Roll out the pastry into a rectangle about 35 x 22.5 cm/14 x 9 inches, then cut out 4 circles about 12.5 cm/5 inches in diameter. Damp the edges of the circles, then place a quarter of the filling on half of each circle. Fold the pastry over, sealing the edges of the pastry together.

❹ Place the turnovers on the prepared baking sheet and brush them with milk. Bake for 25 minutes, or until the pastry is golden. Serve hot or cold.

fish dishes

Aubergine and Tuna Risotto

Fresh tuna is an excellent ingredient in risotto, especially marinated in a mixture of lime and chilli. The sweetness of aubergine balances the dish perfectly.

SERVES 4

- 1 or 2 tuna steaks, weighing 225 g/ 8 oz, cut into 2-cm/1-inch pieces.
- 2 aubergines, cut into 1-cm/½-inch pieces
- 3–4 Tbsp olive oil
- 1 onion, finely chopped
- 250 g/9 oz arborio rice
- 1.2 l/2 pints well-flavoured stock
- 1 Tbsp chopped fresh coriander
- 1 Tbsp chopped fresh parsley
- Parmesan cheese shavings

MARINADE:

- Grated zest and juice of 1 lime
- 6 spring onions, finely sliced
- 1 red chilli, seeded and chopped
- Salt and freshly ground black pepper
- 3 Tbsp fruity olive oil

Preparation time: 40 minutes

Cooking time: 30 minutes

---

❶ Mix all the ingredients for the marinade together in a bowl, then add the tuna, turning the fish over in the mixture. Leave for 30 minutes. Salt layers of aubergines in a colander. Leave for 30 minutes then rinse and dry.

❷ Heat the oil in a large pan. Add the onion and cook until softened, then add the aubergine and continue frying until it just starts to brown.

❸ Stir the rice into the pan juices. Add one-third of the stock to the pan. Bring to the boil, then simmer until nearly all the liquid has been absorbed, stirring frequently, then repeat with half the remaining stock.

❹ Drain the tuna, reserving the marinade, then place under a hot grill for 3 to 4 minutes turning once or twice; it should be starting to brown on the outside but still slightly pink in the middle. Meanwhile, add the remaining stock and reserved marinade to the risotto and simmer as before until the liquid is absorbed.

❺ Add the tuna and any pan juices to the risotto, season to taste, then sprinkle with the chopped herbs and the Parmesan shavings.

Tuna and Aubergine Kebabs

Perfect fish kebabs for the garden or beach barbecue or to grill indoors out of season.

SERVES 4

- 600 g/20 oz fresh tuna steaks, about 2 cm/1 inch thick, cut into 2-cm/1-inch cubes
- 1 long, thin, Japanese-style aubergine

MARINADE:

- Grated zest and juice of 1 lime
- 4 Tbsp olive oil
- 1 garlic clove, crushed
- 2 Tbsp chopped fresh oregano and parsley mixed
- Salt and freshly ground black pepper

Preparation time: 10 minutes
plus 1 hour marinating

Cooking time: 15 minutes

---

❶ Place the tuna in a glass bowl, then add all the marinade ingredients. Stir well and leave for at least 1 hour, stirring once or twice.

❷ Half cook the aubergine on the barbecue or under the grill, until the skin is just starting to wrinkle. Cut into 1-cm/½-inch thick slices.

❸ Soak the kebab sticks to prevent them charring on the grill. Thread the tuna and aubergine on skewers, then brush with the remaining marinade.

❹ Cook over a moderate heat for 5 to 6 minutes on each side, either on the barbecue or under the grill, basting at intervals with any remaining marinade. Serve with a rice salad.

Aubergine with Gingered Crab and Vanilla Pasta

A most unusual and utterly delicious dish inspired by my friend Philip Britten, the Michelin-star chef at the Capital Hotel in London's Knightsbridge. Use lobster in place of the crab if you wish.

SERVES 4

- 5-cm/2-inch piece fresh ginger
- 225 g/8 oz crab meat
- 250 g/9 oz strong white bread flour
- 2 large eggs
- A few drops natural vanilla essence
- 1 vanilla pod, split and seeds removed
- 5–6 Tbsp fragrant olive oil
- 1 aubergine, finely sliced
- 2-cm/1-inch piece fresh ginger, peeled and finely chopped
- 1 tomato, skinned, seeded and chopped
- Salt and white pepper

Preparation time: 20 minutes

Cooking time: 10 minutes

❶ Grate the larger piece of ginger, including the skin, with a coarse grater. Place the crab meat in a bowl. Gather up the shreds of ginger in your hand, then squeeze the juice over the crab. Leave the crab to marinate in the ginger juice.

❷ Prepare the pasta. Put the flour in a bowl and make a well in the centre. Beat the eggs with the vanilla essence and seeds, then pour into the flour. Bind to a stiff dough, then knead thoroughly. Roll out very thinly, or pass the dough through a pasta machine, until thin enough to cut into spaghetti. Drape over a pole or the back of a chair on a cloth to dry until ready to cook.

❸ Bring a large pan of salted water to the boil. Meanwhile, heat the oil in a pan. Add the aubergine and chopped ginger and cook gently until soft and lightly browned. Add the pasta to the boiling water and cook just until it floats to the top of the water again, 1 to 2 minutes. Drain the pasta well and shake it dry.

❹ Add the marinated crab and juice to the aubergine and heat for about 1 minute. Add the pasta and toss the mixture together. Add the chopped tomato and season just before serving.

Roast Monkfish with Aubergine and Wine Sauce

This sounds sophisticated, but is very quick to cook. Use soured cream or natural yogurt if you prefer in the sauce, but I find that ordinary cream reduces more successfully.

SERVES 3

- 1 monkfish tail, weighing about 600 g/1lb 5 oz, filleted
- 2 Tbsp olive oil
- Knob of butter, plus extra for greasing
- Salt and freshly ground black pepper
- 2 tsp wholegrain mustard
- 4 spring onions, sliced
- 1 small aubergine, finely sliced
- 100 ml/3½ fl oz dry white wine
- 2–3 Tbsp fish stock or water
- 150 ml/4 fl oz double cream
- 3 Tbsp chopped chives
- Salt and freshly ground black pepper

Preparation time: 10 minutes

Cooking time: 25 minutes

---

❶ Preheat the oven to 220°C/425°F/ Gas Mark 7. Pull the papery skin away from the monkfish. Heat the oil and butter in a large pan, then quickly fry the fillets on all sides. Place them on a buttered baking sheet, then spread them with the mustard. Roast in the preheated oven for 15 minutes.

❷ Add the spring onions and aubergine to the pan and cook quickly until the aubergine has absorbed the liquid. Add the wine and continue to cook until the aubergine slices are tender. Add the stock and cream, and simmer until the sauce has reduced and thickened. Add the chives and season to taste.

❸ Slice the monkfish fillets into thick medallions and arrange them on warmed serving plates. Spoon the sauce over the fish, and serve with sautéed potatoes and steamed green beans.

fish dishes

Aubergine and Cod Bake

A simple bake with the flavours of the Mediterranean. I like to serve this with a crisp green salad and crusty French bread to mop up the juices.

SERVES 4

- Butter
- Olive oil, for frying
- 1 aubergine, sliced
- 1 large onion, finely sliced
- 1 garlic clove, crushed
- 2 Tbsp capers
- 50 g/1¾ oz black stoned olives, Provençal if possible
- 400 g/14 oz tinned chopped tomatoes
- 1 Tbsp chopped mixed fresh herbs, such as parsley, oregano, marjoram
- Salt and freshly ground black pepper
- Four 175-g/6-oz pieces of thick cod fillet, skinned

Preparation time: 25 minutes

Cooking time: 20 minutes

❶ Preheat the oven to 200°C/400°F/ Gas Mark 6. Butter an ovenproof serving dish

❷ Heat 2 to 3 tablespoons of oil in a large pan and fry the aubergine slices gently until tender but not brown. Drain on paper towels. Add a little more oil to the pan if necessary, then add the onion and cook until softened and just starting to brown. Stir in the garlic, capers and olives, then add the tomatoes, herbs and seasoning to taste. Simmer the sauce for about 5 minutes, until it is slightly thickened and the onion is cooked.

❸ Pour the sauce into the prepared dish, then nestle the cod fillets into it. Cover the fish with the aubergine slices and dot with butter. Place the dish on a baking sheet if it seems very full and likely to bubble over, then bake in the hot oven for 20 minutes, until the aubergine slices are browned. Serve immediately.

fish dishes

Stuffed Trout with Pine Nuts

A simple way of pan-frying trout stuffed with an aubergine paste for a light lunch or supper dish.

SERVES 4

- 1 large aubergine
- 2 spring onions, chopped
- 1 garlic clove, crushed
- 1 Tbsp tomato paste
- Salt and freshly ground black pepper
- 1 Tbsp chopped fresh oregano or flat-leaf parsley
- 1 Tbsp fresh breadcrumbs, if necessary
- 4 trout, weighing about 250g/9 oz each, cleaned and scaled
- **3 Tbsp butter**
- 50 g/1¾ oz pine nuts
- Chopped fresh parsley, to garnish

Preparation time: 40 minutes

Cooking time: 20 minutes

---

❶ Cook the aubergine on a barbecue, under a grill or in a hot oven until the skin is blistered and wrinkled and the flesh is tender, turning from time to time. Cover with a damp cloth and leave for about 10 minutes, then peel off the skin and roughly chop the flesh.

❷ Place the aubergine in a food processor with the spring onions, garlic, tomato paste and seasoning to taste. Blend to a paste, then fold in the chopped oregano. If the aubergine is very juicy you may need to add 1 tablespoon of fresh breadcrumbs to thicken the paste into a stuffing.

❸ Season the trout lightly inside and out. Spoon the aubergine paste into the trout, holding them closed if necessary with wooden cocktail sticks.

❹ Heat the butter in a large pan, then add the trout and cook over a moderate heat for 6 to 8 minutes on each side, according to size. Add the pine nuts to the pan when the fish has had half the cooking time on the second side. Remove the trout to a plate and keep them warm, then continue to stir-fry the pine nuts in the pan juices until they are browned. Spoon the nuts and the juices over the trout and garnish with a little freshly chopped parsley.

fish dishes

Trout with Aubergine and Cranberry Sauce

Aubergine and cranberries present a wonderful, winning combination; the cranberries balance any oiliness from the aubergine or the fish.

SERVES 4

- 4 Tbsp butter
- 2 Tbsp olive oil
- 1 aubergine, cut into 6-mm/¼-inch dice
- 4 rainbow or brown trout, weighing 250–275 g/9–10 oz each
- 25 g/1 oz dried cranberries
- 3 kaffir lime leaves, finely shredded
- 2–3 Tbsp soured cream
- Salt and freshly ground black pepper

Preparation time: 10 minutes

Cooking time: 20 minutes

❶ Heat 3 tablespoons of butter and 1 tablespoon of oil together in a large pan, then add the aubergine. Cook for 3 to 4 minutes until lightly browned, then remove with a slotted spoon and keep warm in an ovenproof dish.

❷ Add the remaining butter and oil to the pan, then add the trout and fry them gently for 5 to 6 minutes on each side. Transfer them to a plate and keep warm in the oven.

❸ Return the aubergine to the pan and add the cranberries with the shredded lime leaves. Cook for 1 to 2 minutes, then add the soured cream. Continue heating until the cream has melted, season to taste, then serve with the sauce spooned over the fish.

Braised Squid with Aubergine

Many people are discouraged from eating squid by the rubbery texture. But when braised, squid is meltingly tender, and lends itself especially well to Chinese cooking.

SERVES 3 TO 4

- 3 Tbsp vegetable oil
- 450 g/1 lb prepared squid, defrosted if frozen, cut into rings and tentacles chopped
- 1 aubergine, sliced
- 1 large green pepper, cored, seeded and cut into large pieces
- 1 large red pepper, cored, seeded and cut into large pieces
- 350 g/12 oz Chinese leaves, cut into thick slices
- 1 large onion, roughly chopped
- 2 Tbsp cornflour
- 250 ml/9 fl oz water
- 100 ml/3½ fl oz sherry
- 100 ml/3½ fl oz soy sauce

Preparation time: 10 minutes

Cooking time: 30 minutes

❶ Heat the oil in a wok, then add the squid and fry quickly for 1 to 2 minutes until it becomes opaque. Remove from the wok with a slotted spoon.

❷ Add the aubergine to the wok and cook until lightly browned, adding a little extra oil if necessary, then add the remaining vegetables. Blend the cornflour with a little of the water, then add to the wok with the remaining water, sherry and soy sauce. Bring to the boil, stirring all the time, then return the squid to the wok and mix with the vegetables.

❸ Cover and simmer gently for 15 minutes. Serve immediately, with plain boiled rice or noodles.

Marinated Swordfish with Aubergine Ribbons

Swordfish readily absorbs the flavours of marinades, and I like to use lime for a really fresh tang. Ribbons of fried aubergine provide an unusual garnish.

SERVES 4

- 4 swordfish steaks, about 1 cm/ ½ inch thick and weighing about 150 g/5 oz each
- 3 Tbsp olive oil
- 1 small long aubergine, halved and sliced into fine ribbons

MARINADE:

- Grated zest and juice of 2 limes
- 3 Tbsp fruity olive oil
- 3 spring onions, finely chopped
- Salt and freshly ground black pepper
- 1 garlic clove, crushed
- 1 Tbsp chopped fresh parsley

Preparation and marinating time: up to 4 hours

Cooking time: 10 minutes

❶ Mix all the ingredients for the marinade in a shallow dish, then add the swordfish. Leave to marinate for 1 to 4 hours, turning the steaks in the mixture once or twice.

❷ Heat the oil in a large pan. Drain the swordfish, reserving the marinade, then fry it quickly in the hot oil, allowing 2 to 3 minutes on each side. Remove the fish from the pan and keep it warm.

❸ Add the marinade to the pan and heat it gently, then add the aubergine ribbons and cook quickly until they are soft and beginning to brown. Arrange the ribbons on the swordfish steaks before serving, spooning any remaining juices over the fish.

fish dishes

Stuffed Mussels

I first discovered the delights of stuffed mussels in Brussels, where they have restaurants that specialize in them. The easiest mussels for stuffing are the large, green-lipped variety. The ones I buy are from New Zealand and very meaty.

SERVES 4

- 20 large green-lipped mussels, on the half shell
- 4 Tbsp olive oil
- 1 large onion, finely chopped
- 1 red chilli, seeded and very finely chopped
- 1 small aubergine, very finely chopped
- 2 garlic cloves, crushed
- Salt and freshly ground black pepper
- 50 g/1¾ oz fresh wholewheat breadcrumbs
- Chopped fresh parsley, to garnish

Preparation time: 20 minutes

Cooking time: 15 minutes

---

❶ Preheat the oven to 220°C/425°F/ Gas Mark 7. Loosen the mussels on the half shells and arrange them on a baking sheet.

❷ Heat the oil in a large pan. Add the onion and chilli and cook until starting to soften, then add the aubergine and garlic. Continue cooking for 5 to 6 minutes, until all the vegetables are soft and lightly browned. Season well, then add the breadcrumbs and mix thoroughly.

❸ Pile a teaspoonful of filling into each shell over the mussel, then bake in the hot oven for 12 to 15 minutes, until piping hot. Serve immediately, garnished with chopped parsley.

fish dishes

Deep-fried Fish with Aubergine Couscous

You can use any firm, white fish fillets for this unusual recipe.

SERVES 4

- 50 ml/2 fl oz olive oil
- 1 aubergine, cut into 6-mm/¼-inch dice
- 1 tsp ground turmeric
- ½ cucumber, cut into 6-mm/¼-inch dice
- 6 spring onions, finely chopped
- 40 g/1½ oz pistachio nuts, roughly chopped
- 50 g/1¾ oz dried apricots, finely chopped
- 350 ml/12 fl oz well-flavoured vegetable stock
- 150 g/5½ oz couscous
- 1 tsp white wine vinegar (optional)
- Vegetable oil, for deep-frying
- 1 large egg white
- 2 Tbsp double cream
- 150 g/5½ oz fine wholewheat flour
- 1 tsp chilli powder
- 2 tsp ground cumin
- Salt and freshly ground black pepper
- 500 g/1 lb 2 oz filleted white fish, cut into 2-cm/1-inch pieces
- Lemon wedges, to garnish

Preparation time: 30 minutes
Cooking time: 10–20 minutes

---

❶ Heat the olive oil in a pan. Add the aubergine and turmeric and fry for 3 to 4 minutes, until soft. Turn into a bowl and add the cucumber, spring onions, nuts and apricots.

❷ Bring the stock to the boil in a small pan, then add the couscous. Cover, remove from the heat and leave for 20 minutes.

❸ Heat the oil for deep-frying in a large pan to 190°C/375°F. Meanwhile, whisk the egg white in a bowl until just frothy, then stir in the cream. Mix the flour on a flat plate with the spices and a little salt and pepper. Toss the fish in the egg and cream, rubbing the mixture into the flesh. Coat the pieces in the seasoned flour.

❹ Deep-fry the fish in 2 to 3 batches for about 3 minutes, then remove with a slotted spoon and drain on paper towels. Keep the cooked fish warm.

❺ Stir the couscous into the vegetables and season well. Add a teaspoon of wine vinegar if you wish. Make a mound of couscous on each plate, then top with the deep-fried fish.

Almond-coated Fishcakes with Thai Salad

Don't be put off by the number of ingredients in this recipe; it is very straightforward and utterly delicious.

SERVES 4 AS A MAIN COURSE, 8 AS AN APPETIZER

- 125 g/4½ oz fresh white breadcrumbs
- 3–4 Tbsp milk
- 1 Tbsp groundnut oil
- 4 spring onions, finely sliced
- 500 g/1 lb 2 oz white fish fillets, skinned and cut into 6-mm/¼-inch dice
- 1 large egg, beaten
- 1–2 Tbsp chopped fresh coriander
- 1 Tbsp chopped fresh parsley
- Salt and white pepper
- 2–3 Tbsp mayonnaise
- 50 g/1¾ oz ground almonds
- 2–3 Tbsp fragrant olive oil

SALAD:

- 2 long, thin Thai aubergines
- 1–2 hot Thai chillies, seeded if preferred, and finely sliced
- 4 spring onions, finely sliced
- 2 Tbsp fish sauce
- Juice of 2 lemons
- ½ piece lemon grass, bruised and finely sliced
- 2 lime leaves, finely shredded – use dried if fresh are not available
- 2 Tbsp caster sugar
- 50 g/1¾ oz mange tout, finely shredded lengthways
- 50 g/1¾ oz baby corn, finely shredded lengthways

Preparation and marinating time: 1 hour

Cooking time: 15 minutes

---

❶ First make the salad. Cook the aubergines on a barbecue, under a grill or in a hot oven, until blackened and wrinkled, turning once or twice. Cover with a damp cloth and leave to cool for about 10 minutes, then peel off the skin. Chop the aubergine into large chunks, then add to all the other salad ingredients in a large bowl and leave to marinate for at least 30 minutes.

❷ Soak 2 cups of the breadcrumbs in the milk for a few minutes, then squeeze them dry and discard the milk. Heat the groundnut oil in a large pan. Add the spring onions and cook until soft but not browned. Remove with a slotted spoon and mix with the breadcrumbs in a large bowl. Add the fish, egg, coriander and parsley. Season to taste, then add just enough mayonnaise to bind the mixture together.

❸ Mix together the remaining breadcrumbs and the ground almonds on a flat plate. Shape the fish mixture into 8 large fishcakes, then coat with the almond breadcrumbs, pressing the coating onto the fishcakes.

❹ Heat the olive oil in the pan, then add the fishcakes and fry gently for 4 to 5 minutes on each side. Serve the fishcakes on a bed of the salad, with some of the salad juices spooned around.

fish dishes

Mediterranean Fish Stew

Making a large casserole of mixed seafood is an expensive business unless you have ready access to fishermen landing their catch on the quayside. Adding an aubergine to the pot makes the fish go much further, and gives a certain sweetness.

SERVES 4

- 4 Tbsp olive oil, plus extra for drizzling
- 1 large onion, chopped
- 1 large aubergine, cut into 2-cm/1-inch cubes
- 250 g/9 oz prepared squid rings
- 100 ml/3½ fl oz dry white wine
- 400 g/14 oz tinned chopped tomatoes
- 1 kg/2 lb 4 oz assorted white fish fillets, skinned and cut into pieces
- 450 ml/16 fl oz well-flavoured fish stock
- Salt and freshly ground black pepper
- 500 g/1 lb 2 oz mussels, scrubbed and debearded
- Grated zest and juice of 1 lemon
- 2 Tbsp chopped fresh flat-leafed parsley
- Toasted French bread or ciabatta, to serve

Preparation time: 15 minutes

Cooking time: 20 minutes

---

❶ Heat the oil in a large deep pan. Add the onion and cook over a low heat for about 4 minutes until softened but not browned. Add the aubergine and squid and fry quickly until all the oil has been absorbed, then add the wine and tomatoes.

Stir the fish into the pan, then add sufficient stock to just cover the fish. Season with salt and pepper, then bring gently to the boil. Cover the pan and cook for 5 to 6 minutes, until the fish is just cooked but not breaking up.

❷ Add the mussels to the pan, return the stew to the boil, then cover and cook for a further 2 to 3 minutes, until all the shells have opened. Discard any that do not open.

❸ Add the lemon zest and juice, then season again if necessary and add the chopped parsley. Serve in deep bowls with slices of toasted bread, and a little extra olive oil drizzled over each serving.

Salmon and Aubergine Kedgeree

I love kedgeree, and have included aubergine and sultanas, and used fresh salmon to provide a good colour contrast to the extra vegetables. Add a splash of cream before serving if you wish, and a spoonful of mango chutney for extra spice.

SERVES 4

- 250 g/9 oz long-grain rice
- Salt and freshly ground black pepper
- 225 g/8 oz salmon fillet, skinned
- 50 g/2 oz butter
- 1 Tbsp curry paste
- 1 onion, sliced
- 1 aubergine, sliced
- 3 Tbsp sultanas
- 3 hard-boiled eggs, chopped

Preparation time: 20 minutes

Cooking time: 15 minutes

❶ Cook the rice in plenty of boiling, salted water for 10 to 12 minutes, until tender. Drain thoroughly in a colander.

❷ Poach the salmon fillet in a pan of barely simmering water for 4 to 5 minutes, until just cooked. Drain the salmon, allow to cool slightly, then flake, removing any bones.

❸ Melt the butter in a large pan with the curry paste. Add the onion and aubergine and cook for about 5 minutes over low heat, until soft. Add a little extra butter if necessary to keep the vegetables moist. Keep the heat low so that the spices do not burn. Add the rice and salmon to the pan, mix carefully and cook gently for 2 minutes.

❹ Add the chopped eggs to the kedgeree with the sultanas, then season to taste. Serve immediately.

Skate with Blackened Aubergine Butter

A variation on a traditional fish dish served with black butter; the aubergine gives just a little more flavour. Use sole or halibut if you prefer.

SERVES 4

- 50 g/2 oz butter
- 2 Tbsp olive oil
- 1 small aubergine, cut into 6-mm/¼-inch dice
- 1 garlic clove, crushed
- 2 Tbsp capers
- 4 wings of skate, weighing about 250 g/9 oz each
- Salt and freshly ground black pepper
- 1 Tbsp chopped fresh parsley
- 2 Tbsp lemon juice

Preparation time: 5 minutes

Cooking time: 15 minutes

---

❶ Heat the butter and oil together in a large pan, then add the aubergine and cook over a moderate heat for 4 to 5 minutes, until softened and starting to brown. Add the garlic and capers and cook for another minute. Remove the vegetables from the pan with a slotted spoon, and keep warm.

❷ Add the skate wings to the pan and cook for 3 to 4 minutes on each side, adding a little more butter only if absolutely necessary. Return the aubergine to the pan just before the fish is ready, season well and add the parsley with the lemon juice.

❸ Serve the skate with the aubergine butter spooned over.

fish dishes

Fish and Aubergine Pie

This is called a fish pie, although there is no pastry or potato topping in sight!
Instead, the topping is made of slices of aubergine over a filling of mixed shellfish
and fillets of plaice. It makes a wonderful summer dish.

SERVES 4

- 2 large aubergines, cut lengthways into 6-mm/¼-inch slices
- Salt and white pepper
- 3 Tbsp butter, plus extra for greasing
- 3 Tbsp plain flour
- 450 ml/16 fl oz milk
- 100 ml/3½ fl oz dry white wine
- 2 Tbsp chopped chives
- 300 g/10½ oz mixed shelled prawns and mussels, defrosted if frozen
- 250 g/9 oz plaice or lemon sole fillets, skinned and cut into 2-cm/1-inch pieces
- 2–3 Tbsp olive oil
- Paprika, for sprinkling

Preparation time: 45 minutes
Cooking time: 25 minutes

---

❶ Arrange the aubergines in a single layer on a baking sheet, then sprinkle them with salt and leave for 30 minutes. Rinse thoroughly in cold water, then pat dry on absorbent kitchen paper.

❷ Preheat the oven to 200°C/400°F/ Gas Mark 6. Melt the butter in a large pan over a moderate heat, then remove from the heat and stir in the flour. Cook gently for 1 minute, then gradually stir in the milk off the heat. Add the wine, then bring the sauce slowly to the boil. Season lightly and add the chives, then stir in the shellfish and plaice. Pour into a buttered ovenproof dish.

❸ Heat a pan and add the olive oil. Cook the aubergine slices in batches until browned on both sides, adding more oil if necessary. Overlap the slices on top of the fish.

❹ Bake the pie in the preheated oven for 20 minutes. Sprinkle with a little paprika before serving with creamy potatoes and green vegetables.

Lamb and Aubergine Curry

Lamb and Aubergine Kebabs

Aubergine Stuffed with Lamb and Couscous

Beef, Aubergine and Pepper Soup

Meatballs with Aubergine and Tomato Sauce

Aubergine Goulash

Aubergine Stuffed with Lamb and Egg

Aubergine and Turkey Burgers

Potted Ham with Aubergine

Spiced Pork and Aubergine Chop Suey

Aubergine Stuffed with Pork and Mushroom

Beef and Aubergine Biryani

Beef with Dates and Aubergine

Rich Aubergine Râgout

Braised Chicken with Aubergine and Prunes

Chicken Moussaka

Roast Chicken with Aubergine Paste

Deep-fried Aubergine and Chicken Strips

Chicken and Aubergine Risotto

Venison Sausage and Aubergine Casserole

Meat and Poultry Dishes

Lamb and Aubergine Curry

Lamb and aubergines both readily absorb spices and seasonings, and are therefore perfect for curries. Try the parathas on page 120 as an additional accompaniment.

SERVES 6

- 100 ml/3½ fl oz vegetable oil or ghee
- 2 aubergines, finely sliced
- 500 g/1 lb 2 oz boneless shoulder or leg of lamb, diced
- 50 g/1¾ oz creamed coconut, crumbled or chopped
- Roughly torn coriander leaves, to garnish

CURRY PASTE:

- 2 large onions, roughly chopped
- 4 garlic cloves, roughly chopped
- 2 green chillies, seeded and chopped
- 5-cm/2-inch piece fresh ginger, peeled and roughly chopped
- 1 Tbsp curry paste or powder
- 2 tsp salt
- 2 Tbsp tomato paste

Preparation time: 15 minutes

Cooking time: 1½ hours

❶ Blend together all the ingredients for the paste in a blender.

❷ Heat the oil in a large pan, then add the aubergine slices and cook over a medium heat for 8 to 10 minutes, until softened and starting to brown. Add the prepared curry paste and cook for 2 to 3 minutes, then stir in the diced lamb. Cook for 3 to 4 minutes over a moderately high heat, until the meat is starting to brown, then add the coconut. Cover the pan and cook slowly for 1 hour, stirring from time to time and adding a little water, if necessary, to prevent the curry from sticking.

❸ Season to taste with salt, then garnish with coriander leaves and serve immediately, with boiled rice or parathas (page 120).

TIP

Side dishes of cucumber sliced in to natural yogurt, or chopped celery and red pepper, served in small bowls or ramekins make attractive accompaniments to spiced dishes.

meat and poultry dishes

70

Lamb and Aubergine Kebabs

The rich juices of the lamb help to moisten and flavour the aubergine in these delicious kebabs. Serve with rice if you prefer, but they make ideal party or barbecue food when served in warm pitta bread.

SERVES 4 TO 6

- 500 g/1 lb 2 oz boned leg or shoulder of lamb, cut into 2-cm/1-inch cubes
- 1 large aubergine, cut into 2-cm/1-inch cubes
- 12 cherry tomatoes

MARINADE:

- Grated zest and juice of 1 lemon
- Grated zest and juice of 1 lime
- 1 Tbsp chopped fresh coriander
- 1 hot red chilli, very finely chopped
- Salt and freshly ground black pepper
- 2 Tbsp olive oil

DRESSING:

- 150 ml/5 fl oz soured cream
- 150 ml/5 fl oz natural yogurt
- 3 Tbsp snipped chives
- 1 Tbsp chopped fresh parsley

Preparation time: 1¼ hours

Cooking time: 15 minutes

---

❶ Place the lamb in a shallow dish. Mix all the ingredients for the marinade together, then pour the mixture over the lamb. Leave to marinate for at least 1 hour.

❷ Place the aubergine in a colander and sprinkle with salt. Leave for at least 30 minutes, then rinse with cold water. Pat dry on paper towels.

❸ Mix all the ingredients for the dressing together, then spoon into a small serving bowl.

❹ Drain the lamb, reserving the marinade, and thread onto 12 kebab skewers with the aubergine and tomatoes. Do not pack the pieces too closely together. Cook the kebabs on a barbecue or under a grill for 12 to 15 minutes, turning occasionally and basting with the reserved marinade, until the lamb and aubergine are browned and tender.

❺ Serve on the skewers or in warmed pitta breads, with a spoonful of the dressing.

Aubergine Stuffed with Lamb and Couscous

A filling baked aubergine recipe that only needs a salad to accompany it. Couscous is easy to cook and makes an excellent stuffing for vegetables.

SERVES 4

- 2 aubergines
- Salt and freshly ground black pepper
- 300 ml/10 fl oz well-flavoured stock
- Good pinch of saffron
- 175 g/6 oz couscous
- 6 green cardamoms, lightly crushed and seeds removed
- 1 tsp ground ginger
- 2 garlic cloves
- 3 Tbsp olive oil, plus extra if necessary
- 1 large onion, finely chopped
- 250 g/9 oz lamb, finely sliced
- 1 green chilli, seeded and chopped
- 100 g/3½ oz ready-to eat dried apricots, finely chopped
- Butter, for greasing

Preparation time: 40 minutes

Cooking time: 40 minutes

---

❶ Cut the aubergines in half lengthways, leaving the stalks to help keep the aubergines in shape during cooking. Cut and scoop out the flesh, leaving a shell about 6-mm/¼-inch thick. Salt the shells lightly, then leave them for 30 minutes upside down on paper towels to drain. Chop the flesh.

❷ Bring the stock to the boil with the saffron, then pour in the couscous. Cover the pan, remove from the heat and leave to stand.

❸ Grind the cardamom seeds, ground ginger and garlic to a rough paste in a pestle and mortar, or with the end of a rolling pin. Preheat the oven to 220°C/425°F/Gas Mark 7.

❹ Heat the oil in a pan, add the onion and spice paste, and cook over a low heat until soft. Add the lamb, chilli, and aubergine flesh, and cook quickly until the lamb has browned, adding a little extra oil if necessary. Stir in the couscous and chopped apricots. Season to taste.

❺ Rinse the aubergine shells thoroughly in cold water, then place in a buttered aluminium ovenproof dish. Pile the filling into the shells, then cover with buttered aluminium foil and bake in the preheated oven for 20 minutes. Remove the foil and cook for a further 10 to 15 minutes, until the top is browned. Serve with a mixed, tossed salad.

Beef, Aubergine and Pepper Soup

A spicy soup with the flavours of the Pacific Rim. I serve this as a lunch or supper dish with bread, but you could add a spoonful of cooked rice to each helping to make it more substantial.

SERVES 4 TO 6

- 125 g/4½ oz boneless stewing steak
- 3 Tbsp groundnut oil
- 1 large onion, finely chopped
- 1 small aubergine, cut into 6-mm/¼-inch dice
- 1 hot red chilli, seeded and very finely chopped
- 1 green pepper, cored, seeded and chopped
- 2-cm/1-inch piece fresh ginger, peeled and finely sliced
- 1 stick lemon grass, bruised and finely chopped
- 3 fresh lime leaves, finely shredded (use dried if fresh are unavailable)
- 1.2l/2 pt well-flavoured stock
- Soy sauce and salt, to taste

Preparation time: 15 minutes

Cooking time: 1 hour

❶ Cut the beef into 1-cm/½-inch strips, then slice it very finely. Heat the oil in a large pan, then add the beef and cook quickly until well browned. Add the onion, aubergine, chilli, pepper, ginger and lemon grass, then cover the pan and cook slowly for 4 to 5 minutes.

❷ Add the lime leaves and stock, then bring to the boil. Cover and simmer for at least 1 hour, until all the ingredients are tender and the flavours have blended.

❸ Season to taste with soy sauce and salt before serving.

Meatballs with Aubergine and Tomato Sauce

Meatballs make a welcome change to the more usual ground beef sauce for pasta. Simmer the meatballs gently to prevent them breaking up during cooking.

SERVES 4

MEATBALLS:

- 500 g/1 lb 2 oz ground lamb
- 6 spring onions, finely chopped
- 100 g/3½ oz fresh wholewheat breadcrumbs
- 1 Tbsp tomato paste
- ½ tsp ground turmeric
- Salt and freshly ground black pepper
- 1 large egg, beaten
- Grated Parmesan cheese, to serve (optional)

SAUCE:

- 3 Tbsp olive oil
- 1 aubergine, cut into 1-cm/½-inch chunks
- 1 onion, finely diced
- 1 garlic clove, finely sliced
- ½ tsp ground turmeric
- 1 tsp ground cumin
- 400 g/14 oz tinned chopped tomatoes
- 1 bay leaf
- Salt and freshly ground black pepper
- 8–10 fresh basil leaves, torn

Preparation time: 25 minutes

Cooking time: 30 minutes

---

❶ Mix all the ingredients for the meatballs together. Shape the mixture with wet hands into walnut-sized balls.

❷ To make the sauce, heat the oil in a large pan, then add the eggplant and fry gently until lightly golden. Add the meatballs, together with the onion, garlic, turmeric and cumin, and cook until the meatballs are browned all over. Add extra oil only if the meatballs are sticking.

❸ Add the tomatoes and bay leaf with salt and pepper, and bring the mixture to the boil. Simmer gently for 20 minutes, then season to taste. Add the basil just before serving.

❹ Serve with pasta, sprinkling a little grated Parmesan over the meatballs if wished.

meat and poultry dishes

Aubergine Goulash

Perhaps this isn't a true goulash, but paprika works well with aubergine.

SERVES 4 TO 6

- 3 Tbsp olive oil
- 1 large onion, finely chopped
- 1 Tbsp caraway seeds
- 750 g/1 lb 10 oz boneless shoulder or leg of pork, cut into 2-cm/1-inch pieces
- 2 Tbsp sweet paprika
- 1 green and 1 red pepper, seeded and cut into 4-cm/1½-inch pieces
- 1 aubergine, cut into 4-cm/1½-inch pieces
- 2 garlic cloves, finely sliced
- 400 g/14 oz tinned chopped tomatoes
- 600 ml/1 pt well-flavoured stock
- Salt and freshly ground black pepper

Preparation time: 25 minutes

Cooking time: 2 hours

❶ Preheat the oven to 160°C/325°F/ Gas Mark 3. Heat the oil in a pan, then cook the onion and caraway seeds slowly for 5 to 6 minutes over a low heat, until the onions are soft but not browned. Dust the pork with the paprika, then add to the pan and cook over a slightly higher heat until the pork has browned. Do not cook too quickly or the paprika will burn.

❷ Add the peppers, aubergine and garlic, and continue cooking slowly for about 2 minutes, until the vegetables are just starting to soften, then add the tomatoes and stock. Season well with salt and pepper, then cover the casserole and cook in the preheated oven for 2 hours.

❸ Season the casserole to taste and serve with boiled rice or noodles.

Aubergine Stuffed with Lamb and Egg

A delicious and unusual light lunch or supper dish. Serve with boiled rice, pilaf or saffron-flavoured couscous.

SERVES 4

- 2 aubergines
- Salt and freshly ground black pepper
- 2 Tbsp olive oil
- 1 large onion, finely chopped
- 500 g/1 lb 2 oz ground lamb
- 2 tsp ground cumin
- 1 tsp ground allspice
- 2 garlic cloves, crushed
- 1 Tbsp tomato paste
- 2 hard-boiled eggs, roughly chopped
- 2 Tbsp capers, rinsed
- Butter, for greasing

Preparation time: 40 minutes

Cooking time: 20 minutes

❶ Preheat the oven to 220°C/425°F/ Gas Mark 7. Cut the aubergines in half lengthways through the stalks. Scoop out the flesh, leaving a shell about 6-mm/¼-inch thick. Salt the aubergines, then leave them to drain upside down for 30 minutes. Roughly chop the flesh.

❷ Heat the oil in a pan, add the onion and cook gently until soft. Add the lamb, cumin, ground allspice and garlic and cook until the lamb has browned. Stir in the tomato paste, then cover and cook for 10 minutes. Add the egg and capers, then season the filling well. Rinse the shells, then pat them dry.

❸ Place the shells in a buttered oven-proof dish, then fill with the lamb and egg mixture. Cover the dish with foil, then bake for 20 minutes.

Aubergine and Turkey Burgers

My husband thought there ought to be a burger recipe in this book, so here it is! I have tried to conjure up the flavours of Italy, using dolcelatte in the burgers and ciabatta rolls to hold them. Don't fry the aubergine slices in too much oil, so that they are very juicy, or the burgers will become soft and very difficult to eat.

Serves 4

- 4 ciabatta rolls
- 400 g/14 oz lean, boned turkey or chicken, cut into strips
- 4 spring onions, roughly chopped
- 75 g/2¾ oz crumbled dolcelatte or other blue cheese
- 4 halves sun-dried tomatoes, roughly chopped
- 2 garlic cloves
- Salt and freshly ground black pepper
- Olive oil, for frying
- 4 large, thick aubergine slices
- Lettuce leaves
- Mustard or mayonnaise, for serving

Preparation time: 15 minutes

Cooking time: 10 minutes

❶ Warm the rolls in a low oven. Process the turkey, spring onions, cheese, tomatoes and garlic to a paste in a food processor, in 2 batches if necessary. Season the mixture, then shape into 4 flat burgers.

❷ Heat 1 to 2 tablespoons of olive oil in a large pan and add the burgers and aubergine slices. Fry gently for 4 to 5 minutes on each side, adding extra oil only if the burgers are sticking.

❸ Split the warm rolls and place a slice of aubergine in the bottom of each. Top with a burger, some lettuce and a dollop of mayonnaise or mustard. Cover with the top of the roll, then enjoy!

meat and poultry dishes

Potted Ham with Aubergines

A rich mousse, set in individual moulds lined with aubergine slices. Serve with lots of salad and fresh toast.

SERVES 4

- 2 large aubergines
- Salt and freshly ground black pepper
- 750 ml/5 fl oz milk
- 1 Tbsp butter
- 1 Tbsp plain flour
- 2 tsp Dijon or pepper mustard
- Olive oil, for frying and greasing
- 4 Tbsp dry white wine
- 1 tsp powdered gelatine
- 150 g/5½ oz cooked chopped ham
- 150 ml/5 fl oz double cream
- 2 Tbsp chopped fresh parsley

Preparation time: 1½ hours

Cooking time: 2 hours

---

❶ Slice one aubergine very thinly. Lay the slices on a baking sheet in a single layer, sprinkle with salt, then leave for 30 minutes. Cook the other aubergine over a barbecue, under a grill or in a hot oven until the skin is wrinkled and blistered and the flesh is tender; turn once or twice during cooking. Cover with a damp cloth and leave for about 10 minutes, then peel off the skin.

❷ Heat the milk, butter and flour together in a pan until thickened and boiling, stirring all the time. Add the mustard, salt and pepper, then remove from the heat, cover with waxed paper to prevent a skin forming, and leave until cold.

❸ Rinse the salted aubergine thoroughly and pat dry on paper towels. Heat a pan, add a little oil, then cook the slices on both sides, a few at a time, until tender, adding more oil as necessary. Drain on paper towels and leave to cool.

❹ Heat the wine in a small pan until bubbling, then remove from the heat and sprinkle on the gelatine. Stir to dissolve, then leave for 2 to 3 minutes. Oil 4 individual bowls and line them with the aubergine slices, overlapping them slightly around the sides.

❺ Cut the peeled aubergine into chunks, then purée it with the ham in a blender or food processor. Whip the cream until thick and floppy. Mix the cream and the ham mixture into the sauce, blending well. Season with pepper; the ham should provide all the salt required. Stir the gelatine again, then fold it into the ham cream with half the parsley.

❻ Carefully spoon the ham into the prepared moulds, banging them on the worktop to shake the mixture down. Chill for at least 2 hours before turning out the moulds onto individual plates. Sprinkle with the remaining parsley and serve with toast and salad.

Spiced Pork and Aubergine Chop Suey

A spicy, Chinese-style dish of marinated pork and crispy, stir-fried vegetables. Make up your own vegetable mix, or use prepared stir-fry vegetables from the supermarket if you are in a hurry. Serve with boiled rice or thread egg noodles.

SERVES 4

- 1 pork tenderloin, weighing about 500 g/1 lb 2 oz
- 600 g/1 lb 5 oz mixed stir-fry vegetables, such as celery, carrot, peppers, mange tout, beansprouts
- 1 aubergine, halved lengthways and sliced thinly
- 4 Tbsp groundnut oil

MARINADE:

- 5-cm/2-inch piece fresh ginger, roughly grated
- 1–2 garlic cloves, crushed
- 1 Tbsp five-spice powder
- 1 green chilli, seeded and very finely chopped
- 4 Tbsp soy sauce
- 1 Tbsp chilli sauce
- 1 Tbsp demerara sugar

Preparation and marinating time:
1¼ hours
Cooking time: 10 minutes

❶ Trim the pork and cut it into very thin slices. Squeeze the juice from the grated ginger and mix it with the other marinade ingredients, then add the pork and toss the slices in the mixture. Leave to stand for at least 1 hour, turning occasionally.

❷ Meanwhile, prepare the vegetables for the stir-fry, cutting them all into thin 5-cm/2-inch lengths.

❸ Heat the oil in a wok or a large pan until almost smoking, then add the pork and aubergine. Stir-fry until both are well browned, about 4 minutes, then add the remaining vegetables. Continue to cook for a further 2 to 3 minutes, adding any remaining marinade. Serve immediately.

Aubergine Stuffed with Pork and Mushroom

Use small purple or striped aubergines for this dish, if available. I like to make a fresh tomato sauce to serve with it, making full use of the hot oven while it is on to bake the aubergines.

SERVES 4

- 4 small aubergines, round ones if possible, or 2 larger ones
- Salt
- 4 Tbsp olive oil
- 1 large onion, finely chopped
- 4 rashers unsmoked back bacon, chopped
- 1 garlic clove, crushed
- 250 g/9 oz ground pork
- 1 tsp paprika
- 125 g/4½ oz mushrooms
- Salt and freshly ground black pepper
- 1 Tbsp tomato paste
- 8–12 basil leaves, roughly torn
- Stock, wine or water
- Chopped fresh basil, to garnish

SAUCE:

- 8 ripe tomatoes, halved
- 1 small onion, quartered
- 2 garlic cloves, peeled but left whole
- 1 Tbsp demerara sugar
- Olive oil, to drizzle

Preparation time: 30 minutes

Cooking time: 40 minutes

❶ Preheat the oven to 240°C/450°F/ Gas Mark 9. Cut off the tops of the aubergines, if using round ones, and scoop out the flesh, leaving a shell about 6 mm/¼ inch thick. If using oval aubergines, halve them, and scoop out the flesh. Salt lightly, then leave the shells for about 20 minutes upside down on paper towels to drain. Chop the flesh fine.

❷ Heat the oil in a pan. Add the onion and cook over a low heat with the bacon and garlic for about 5 minutes, then add the ground pork and paprika. Cook quickly until browned, then add half the eggplant flesh and mushrooms and cook for a further 2 to 3 minutes.

❸ Season the mixture, adding the tomato paste and basil. Add a little stock, wine or water, if necessary, to moisten the mixture, then leave to simmer gently. Rinse the aubergine shells thoroughly in cold water and drain. Pack the filling into them, then place in a buttered ovenproof dish. Cover with aluminium foil.

❹ Arrange the sauce ingredients in a single layer in a roasting pan with the remaining aubergine flesh. Season well, adding the sugar and a drizzle of olive oil. Cook the sauce at the top of the oven with the aubergines underneath for 35 to 40 minutes, until the tomatoes have started to blacken.

❺ Remove the sauce ingredients from the oven and allow to cool slightly. Remove the foil from the aubergines and return to the oven until the sauce is completed. Tip all the roasted vegetables and their juices into a blender and process until smooth. Press the purée through a sieve with the back of a spoon to give a smooth sauce, then season to taste. Serve the stuffed aubergines with the tomato sauce, sprinkled with the chopped basil.

meat and poultry dishes

81

Beef and Aubergine Biryani

A wonderful spicy dish for lazy entertaining. Most of it can be prepared in advance and heated through at the last moment. For special occasions decorate with gold or silver leaf just before serving.

SERVES 6

- 6 Tbsp ghee or sunflower oil
- 500 g/1 lb 2 oz braising steak, cut into 2-cm/1-inch pieces, or 500 g/ 1 lb 2 oz cooked diced beef
- 2 bay leaves
- 350 g/12 oz Basmati rice, rinsed
- 2 large onions, finely sliced
- 1 tsp curry paste
- 50 g/1¾ oz sultanas
- 50 g/1¾ oz creamed coconut, finely chopped

CURRY SAUCE:

- 2 onions, roughly chopped
- 3 garlic cloves, roughly chopped
- 1 green chilli, seeded and chopped
- 1 Tbsp mild curry paste
- 2 Tbsp tomato paste
- 1 Tbsp demerara sugar
- 6 Tbsp ghee or sunflower oil
- 1 large aubergine, cut into 1-cm/½-inch dice
- 300 ml/10 fl oz single cream
- Salt
- 2–3 Tbsp chopped fresh coriander

GARNISHES:

- 2 hard-boiled eggs, quartered
- 50 g/1¾ oz whole blanched almonds, fried until golden brown
- 2–3 tomatoes, sliced

Preparation time: 2½ hours

Cooking time: 30 minutes

---

❶ Preheat the oven to 160°C/325°F/ Gas Mark 3. Heat 3 tablespoons of the ghee or oil in a flameproof casserole, brown the meat, then add enough water to cover. Add the bay leaves, then bring just to the boil. Cover the casserole and cook in the preheated oven for approximately 2 hours.

❷ Rinse the rice then bring to the boil in a large pan of cold water. Stir, then cover and cook for 10 minutes. Drain and rinse thoroughly, then drain again.

❸ Prepare the curry sauce. Blend the onions, garlic and chilli with the curry paste, tomato paste and sugar in a blender or food processor. Heat the oil in a large pan, add the aubergine and cook until starting to brown, then add the curry sauce and continue to fry gently for 4 to 5 minutes. Stir in the cream and bring almost to a gentle simmer, then add salt to taste. Remove from the heat, and set aside ready to reheat at the last moment.

❹ Heat the remaining ghee or oil in a large pan or wok, add the onions and cook until golden. Remove half with a slotted spoon, to use as garnish. Add the curry paste to the onions and cook for a further minute, then add 3 tablespoons of juices from the meat, or water, and cook for 1 minute longer.

❺ Drain the meat and add it to the pan, or add the leftover cooked meat if using. Stir-fry until it is well heated through and has absorbed the juices. Once hot, add the cooked rice to the pan with the chopped coconut and stir gently until piping hot. Reheat the sauce gently and add the coriander.

❻ Serve the biryani decorated with the prepared garnishes, with the curry sauce spooned over.

Beef with Dates and Aubergine

This is my interpretation of a tagine, the stew from North Africa which is always sweetened either with dates, figs, prunes or apricots, or with sugar or honey.

SERVES 6

- 5–6 Tbsp olive oil
- 6 pieces of braising steak, each weighing about 250 g/9 oz
- 2 large onions, sliced
- 2 garlic cloves, finely sliced
- 2 tsp ground cumin
- 1 tsp ground turmeric
- 1 large cinnamon stick
- 6 cloves
- 400 g/14 oz tinned chopped tomatoes
- Salt and freshly ground black pepper
- 150 g/5½ oz dried stoned dates
- 400 ml/14 fl oz well-flavoured stock
- 1 large aubergine, cut into thin slices

Preparation and salting time:

1 hour

Cooking time: 3½ hours

---

❶ Preheat the oven to 160°C/325°F/ Gas Mark 3. Heat 4 tablespoons of oil in a large flameproof casserole, then add the beef and fry quickly on both sides until browned. Remove with a slotted spoon and leave on a plate.

❷ Add a little extra oil to the casserole if necessary, then add the onions, garlic and spices and cook

until soft but not browned. Stir in the tomatoes, then season with salt and pepper and add the dates. Bury the meat back in the pan amongst the vegetables, then add sufficient stock to cover the meat. Bring gently to the boil, then cover the casserole and cook in the preheated oven for 2 to 2½ hours, until the beef is tender.

❸ Meanwhile, layer the aubergine slices in a colander, salting them well, then leave for 45 minutes. Rinse the slices thoroughly in cold water and pat them dry on paper towels.

❹ When the meat is tender, season the casserole to taste, then arrange the aubergine slices over the top and brush them liberally with olive oil. Raise the oven temperature to 180°C/350°F/Gas Mark 4 then bake the casserole, uncovered, for a further 30 to 40 minutes, until the aubergine slices are browned. Serve with cucumber and yogurt salad.

Rich Aubergine Râgout

There are spaghetti sauces, and then there are rich, flavoursome râgouts. I use a mixture of meats for this sauce, and add aubergine for extra richness. Serve with spaghetti, tagliatelle or any flat pasta.

Serves 6 to 8

- 4 Tbsp olive oil
- 1 large onion, finely chopped
- 1 aubergine, cut into 1-cm/½-inch chunks
- 250--300 g/9–10½ oz ground beef
- 250–300 g/9–10½ oz ground pork
- 250 g/9 oz chicken livers, finely chopped
- 150 ml/5 fl oz red wine
- 2 400 g/14 oz tinned chopped tomatoes
- 1 Tbsp tomato paste
- 2 garlic cloves, finely sliced
- 2–3 bay leaves
- Salt and freshly ground black pepper
- Freshly grated nutmeg, to taste

Preparation time: 25 minutes

Cooking time: 2 hours
---

❶ Heat half the olive oil in a large pan. Add the onion and cook for 4 to 5 minutes over a low heat until soft and transparent. Add the remaining oil and the aubergine, then cook quickly until the aubergine starts to brown. Stir in the meat and chicken livers, and continue cooking over a medium high heat until all the meat is browned.

❷ Pour the wine into the pan and continue cooking over a high heat until the wine has almost evaporated, stirring all the time. Lower the heat, then add all the remaining ingredients. Bring to the boil, then cook for at least 1 hour at a very slow simmer. If preferred, cover the pan and cook at 160°C/325°F/Gas Mark 3.

❸ Season the râgout to taste. Serve as a pasta sauce with spaghetti or tagliatelle, use as a sauce for lasagne, or top with creamy potatoes mashed with olive oil and garlic for a baked pie with a difference!

meat and poultry dishes

Braised Chicken with Aubergine and Prunes

A most unusual casserole with a refreshing tang of lemon. I sometimes add ground cumin and ginger to the chicken when frying, but I really think the flavour relies on the brandy, lemon juice and bay.

SERVES 4

- 2 aubergines
- 3 Tbsp olive oil
- 4 chicken pieces
- 1 large onion, finely sliced
- 2 large carrots, thickly sliced
- 150 ml/5 fl oz brandy
- Grated zest and juice of 2 lemons
- 125 g/4½ oz stoned prunes
- Salt and freshly ground black pepper
- 2 large bay leaves
- 300 ml/10 fl oz chicken stock
- Sugar
- Chopped fresh parsley, to garnish

Preparation time: 40 minutes

Cooking time: 1 hour

---

❶ Preheat the oven to 160ºC/325°F/ Gas Mark 3. Cook the aubergines over a barbecue, under a grill or in a hot oven until the skins have wrinkled and blistered and the flesh is tender. Turn once or twice during cooking. Cover with a damp cloth and leave for about 10 minutes to cool, then peel off the skin and roughly chop the aubergine flesh.

❷ Meanwhile, heat the oil in a flameproof casserole and quickly brown the chicken pieces on all sides. Add the onion and carrots and continue cooking for 3 to 4 minutes over a low heat. Heat the brandy in a large metal ladle until it ignites, then pour over the chicken, off the heat, and leave until the flames subside.

❸ Add the lemon zest to the chicken with the aubergine, prunes and seasonings, then add just enough stock to cover the chicken. Bring the casserole to the boil, then cover and cook in the preheated oven for 1 hour, or until the chicken is tender and cooked through.

❹ Remove the bay leaves from the casserole, add the lemon juice, then season the chicken to taste, adding a little sugar if necessary. Garnish the casserole with chopped parsley just before serving. Creamy mashed potatoes would make an ideal accompaniment to the rich sauce.

meat and poultry dishes

Chicken Moussaka

Moussaka is one of the classic aubergine dishes, and I think that this is the best moussaka recipe that I have ever tasted! I use a covered pan to start the sauce as I find that less oil is required if the onion is half steamed in its own juices.

SERVES 4 TO 6

- 100 ml/3½ fl oz olive oil
- 2 large onions, chopped
- 500 g/1 lb 2 oz boneless chicken, finely diced
- 1–2 garlic cloves, crushed
- 150 ml/5 fl oz red wine
- 400 g/14 oz tinned chopped tomatoes
- 2 Tbsp freshly chopped oregano, plus extra for garnish
- Salt and freshly ground black pepper
- 1 Tbsp tomato paste
- 2 large aubergines, sliced
- Butter, for greasing

TOPPING

- 250 g/9 oz ricotta cheese
- 100 g/3½ oz soft goat's cheese with garlic and herbs
- 150 ml/5 fl oz natural yogurt

Preparation time: 1 hour

Cooking time: 30 minutes

---

❶ Heat 2 tablespoons of the oil in a pan, add the onions, cover and cook gently until soft. Remove the lid and stir in the chicken with the garlic. Cook quickly until the chicken changes colour. Add the wine, and cook until it has reduced by half. Add all the other ingredients, then simmer slowly for 30 to 40 minutes, until rich and thick.

❷ Preheat the oven to 220°C/425°F/ Gas Mark 7. Add 3 to 4 tablespoons of the oil to a pan. Fry the aubergine slices a few at a time until browned on both sides, adding more oil as necessary. Remove with a slotted spoon and drain on paper towels.

❸ Layer the chicken sauce and aubergine slices in a buttered, oven-proof dish, finishing with a layer of aubergine. Blend the cheeses and yogurt together into a sauce, add salt and pepper to taste, and spoon the mixture over the aubergines. Bake for 25 to 30 minutes. Serve sprinkled with chopped oregano.

Roast Chicken with Aubergine Paste

A smoky aubergine paste forced under the skin of a chicken before roasting helps to keep it moist. A little ground turmeric adds extra colour and spice.

SERVES 4 TO 6

- 1 aubergine
- Salt and freshly ground black pepper
- 2 carrots, cut into chunks
- 1 onion, cut in wedges
- 2 large courgettes, cut into chunks
- 1 green pepper, cored, seeded and cut into large pieces
- 1 garlic clove, halved
- Olive oil, for drizzling
- 1 chicken, about 1.6 kg/3½ lb
- Pinch of ground turmeric

Preparation time: 40 minutes

Cooking time: 1½ hours

---

❶ Cook the aubergine over a barbecue, under a very hot grill or in a hot oven until the skin is wrinkled and blistered and the flesh is tender. Turn once or twice during cooking. Cover with a damp cloth and leave for about 10 minutes, until cool enough to handle. Peel off the skin, then mash the flesh with salt and pepper to a smooth paste.

❷ Meanwhile, preheat the oven to 200°C/400°F/Gas Mark 6. Place the vegetables and garlic in a roasting pan. Season them lightly and drizzle with olive oil. Carefully loosen the skin on the chicken breast and spread the breast with the aubergine paste, pushing it underneath the skin. Pat the skin back into position. Season the chicken well and sprinkle with a pinch of turmeric. Place the chicken on top of the vegetables.

❸ Roast in the preheated oven for 1 hour, or until the juices run clear when you insert a skewer into the thigh. Remove the chicken, wrap it in foil and leave to stand for 20 minutes before carving. Meanwhile, return the vegetables to the oven to continue roasting for 20 minutes.

❹ Carve the chicken, or cut it into portions, and serve together with the roasted vegetables.

Deep-fried Aubergine and Chicken Strips

A good supper dish to serve with a fine dollop of tartare sauce or mayonnaise and accompanied with an excitingly dressed mixed green salad.

SERVES 4

- 1 egg white
- 1 Tbsp double cream
- Vegetable oil, for deep-frying
- 1 large aubergine, cut into thin strips
- 2 large chicken breasts, cut into thin strips
- 3 Tbsp sesame seeds
- Salt
- Sliced lemon and mayonnaise, to serve

SPICED FLOUR:

- 50 g/1¾ oz fine wholewheat flour
- 2 tsp ground cinnamon
- 2 tsp paprika
- 1 tsp salt

Preparation time: 25 minutes

Cooking time: 15 minutes

❶ Mix the flour with the spices and salt in a shallow dish. Beat the egg white until just frothy, then mix it with the cream.

❷ Heat the oil for deep-frying to 190°C/375°F in a large pan. Dip the aubergine and chicken strips in the cream mixture, then turn them in the seasoned flour to coat well.

❸ Deep-fry the aubergine and chicken in batches until golden, then remove with a slotted spoon and drain on paper towels. Scatter with sesame seeds and salt, and serve with sliced lemon and mayonnaise.

Chicken and Aubergine Risotto

I love risottos and this one has all my favourite ingredients: moist chicken, smoky, mysterious aubergine, and fragrant saffron. A good risotto should be moist and the rice should still have a little bite in the middle. I serve the aubergine as a sauce on top of the risotto, and it works very well indeed.

SERVES 4

- 1 large aubergine
- 1 Tbsp lemon juice
- Good pinch of saffron strands
- 1.2 1/2 pt well-flavoured chicken stock
- 3 Tbsp olive oil
- 1 large onion, finely chopped
- 2–3 celery sticks, finely sliced
- 2 chicken breast fillets, finely diced
- 2 garlic cloves, finely sliced
- 250 g/9 oz arborio rice
- 2 Tbsp fresh flat-leaf parsley
- Salt and freshly ground black pepper
- 1 Tbsp fresh tomato paste or ketchup, optional
- 150 ml/5 fl oz dry white wine
- 2–3 tomatoes, skinned, seeded and chopped

Preparation time: 30 minutes

Cooking time: 40 minutes

---

❶ Cook the aubergine over a barbecue, under a grill or in a hot oven until the skin is wrinkled and blistered and the flesh is tender. Turn once or twice during cooking. Cover with a damp cloth and leave for about 10 minutes to cool slightly, then peel off the skin. Plunge the flesh into a bowl of water with a tablespoon of lemon juice, to prevent discoloration, and leave until required. Soak the saffron strands in the hot stock.

❷ Heat the olive oil in a large pan over a moderate heat, add the onion and celery and cook until soft but not browned, then add the chicken. Cook over a slightly higher heat until the chicken is white all over, then add the garlic and the rice, tossing them in the pan juices.

❸ Add about one-third of the stock to the pan, then bring to the boil, and simmer, stirring frequently, until all the stock has been absorbed. Add half the remaining stock and repeat the simmering.

❹ Drain the aubergine and squeeze with your hands, extracting as much liquid as possible, then chop the flesh roughly and blend it with the parsley and seasonings to a smooth paste. Add a tablespoon of tomato paste or ketchup for colour.

❺ Stir the wine into the risotto, then add the remaining stock and continue cooking until it has a creamy consistency. Add the chopped tomatoes just before the risotto is ready, and season to taste with salt and pepper.

❻ Serve on warmed plates, topped with a spoonful of the smoky aubergine paste.

91

Venison Sausage and Aubergine Casserole

I like to use venison sausages for this casserole, but if these are not available you can use any herby or spicy sausages.

Serves 4

- 2 Tbsp olive oil
- 8 thick venison sausages
- 2 slices smoked bacon, diced
- 1 large onion, finely chopped
- 1 carrot, diced
- 1–2 garlic cloves, sliced
- 150 ml/5 fl oz red wine
- 1 large aubergine, cut into 1-cm/½-inch chunks
- 400 g/14 oz tinned chopped tomatoes
- 100 g/3½ oz Puy lentils
- 1 Tbsp tomato paste
- 300 ml/10 fl oz beef stock
- Salt and freshly ground black pepper

Preparation time: 15 minutes

Cooking time: 1 hour

---

❶ Preheat the oven to 180°C/350°F/ Gas Mark 4. Heat the oil in a flame-proof casserole, then add the sausages and cook them briefly until browned all over. Add the bacon, onion, carrot and garlic, then cover the casserole and cook slowly for 4 to 5 minutes.

❷ Add the red wine, then cook rapidly until it is well reduced. Add all the remaining ingredients, then bring to the boil. Cover and cook in the preheated oven for 1 hour.

❸ Season, and serve from the pot.

Aubergine and Peppers, Szechuan-style

Aubergine and Cracked Wheat Pilaf

Aubergine and Kidney Bean Chilli

Aubergine and Almond Rissoles

Aubergine Olives with Nuts and Cheese

Mixed Vegetable Gumbo

Aubergine with Garlic and Tomatoes

Imam Bayaldi

Spaghetti with Aubergine and Courgettes

Vegetable Loaf

Aubergine Stuffed with Mushroom and Egg

Aubergine and Sweet Potato Curry

Lentil Moussaka

Nut and Aubergine Sausages

Aubergine and Tomato Gratin

Aubergine and Tomato Galette

Aubergine and Wild Rice Bake

Tortillas Stuffed with Aubergine and Chilli

Chickpea and Aubergine Stew

Aubergine and Peppers, Szechuan-style

Szechuan cooking is very spicy. You could serve this as a main course by itself, with boiled or fried rice as an accompaniment, or with a meat or fish dish.

SERVES 3 TO 4

- Groundnut oil, for frying
- 1 large aubergine, cut into 2-cm/ 1-inch chunks
- 2 garlic cloves, crushed
- 5-cm/2-inch piece fresh ginger, peeled and very finely chopped
- 1 onion, roughly chopped
- 2 green peppers, cored, seeded and cut into 2-cm/1-inch pieces
- 1 red pepper, cored, seeded and cut into 2-cm/1-inch pieces
- 1 hot red chilli, seeded and finely shredded
- 100 ml/3½ fl oz well-flavoured vegetable stock
- 1 Tbsp sugar
- 1 tsp rice or white wine vinegar
- Salt and freshly ground black pepper
- 1 tsp cornflour
- 1 Tbsp light soy sauce
- Sesame oil, for sprinkling

Preparation time: 10 minutes

Cooking time: 15 minutes

---

❶ Heat 3 tablespoons of oil in a wok. Add the aubergine and stir-fry for 4 to 5 minutes, until lightly browned. Add more oil if necessary. Remove the aubergine with a slotted spoon and keep warm.

❷ Add a little more oil to the wok, then add the garlic and ginger, and fry for just a few seconds before adding the onions and peppers with the chilli. Stir-fry for 2 to 3 minutes, then return the aubergine to the wok. Mix the remaining ingredients together and add to the wok.

❸ Continue to stir-fry until the sauce has boiled and thickened. Check the seasoning, adding a little more salt or soy sauce as necessary, then serve immediately, sprinkled with sesame oil.

Aubergine and Cracked Wheat Pilaf

I love to cook with cracked wheat as it retains a grainy texture and a nutty flavour. Use whatever vegetables you have to hand, but I find the combination of aubergine, fennel and peppers works very well indeed.

SERVES 4

- 2–3 Tbsp olive oil
- 1 large onion, chopped
- 1 fennel bulb, trimmed and sliced
- 1 aubergine, cut into large dice
- 1 green pepper, cored, seeded and chopped
- 250 g/9 oz cracked wheat or bulghar wheat
- 400 g/14 oz tinned chopped tomatoes
- 700 ml/1¼ pt well-flavoured stock
- Salt and freshly ground black pepper

Preparation time: 15 minutes

Cooking time: 20 minutes

---

❶ Heat the oil in a large pan, add the onion and fennel and cook until just starting to soften. Stir in the aubergine and pepper, then cook for a minute or so before adding the wheat. Add the tomatoes and stock, then bring the pilaf to the boil.

❷ Simmer for 15 to 20 minutes, until the stock has been absorbed. Season well with salt and pepper, then serve with a crisp green salad.

vegetable dishes

Aubergine and Kidney Bean Chilli

Eggplants make a good alternative to lentils for a vegetable-based chilli sauce. The spicing in this is quite strong; use a little less chilli powder if you prefer. Serve with brown rice or tortilla chips, and an avocado dip.

Serves 4

- 3 Tbsp groundnut oil
- 1 large onion, chopped
- 2 tsp chilli powder
- 1 tsp ground cumin
- 1 large aubergine, cut into 1-cm/½-inch chunks
- 1–2 garlic cloves, crushed
- 1 large cinnamon stick
- 2 bay leaves
- 680 g/1 lb 8 oz puréed tomatoes or thick tomato juice
- Salt and freshly ground black pepper
- 400 g/14 oz tinned red kidney beans and juice
- Boiled rice, to serve
- Soured cream and fresh coriander leaves, to garnish

Preparation time: 10 minutes

Cooking time: 40 minutes

---

❶ Heat the oil in a large pan. Add the onion with the chilli powder and cumin and cook for 4 to 5 minutes over a low heat, until the onion is soft but not browned. It is important to cook the onion slowly so that the spices do not burn.

❷ Add the aubergine and garlic, and cook for 1 to 2 minutes, then add the cinnamon and bay leaves with the puréed tomatoes or tomato juice. Add salt and pepper, then bring to the boil. Cover the pan and simmer the sauce slowly for 10 minutes, then add the kidney beans and their juice. Continue cooking for a further 10 minutes, then remove the cinnamon and bay leaves.

❸ Season the chilli to taste, then serve on a bed of rice with a large spoonful of soured cream, garnished with coriander.

Aubergine and Almond Rissoles

Rissole is a very old-fashioned word, but I love these little patties with a side salad and tartare sauce, or even tomato ketchup.

SERVES 4

- 1 large aubergine
- 150 ml/5 fl oz milk
- 1 Tbsp butter
- 1 heaped Tbsp fine wholewheat flour, plus extra for flouring
- Salt and freshly ground black pepper
- 4 spring onions, finely chopped
- 1 Tbsp chopped fresh oregano
- 50 g/¾ oz ground almonds
- 100 g/3½ oz fresh wholewheat breadcrumbs
- 100 ml/3½ oz olive oil
- 2 eggs, beaten
- 75 g/2¾ oz dry wholewheat breadcrumbs, toasted – you will need more if you make your own toasted crumbs
- Tartare sauce and salad, to serve

Preparation time: 1 hour

Cooking time: 15 minutes

---

❶ Cook the aubergine on a barbecue, under a grill or in a hot oven until the skin is wrinkled and blistered and the flesh is tender, turning once or twice. Cover with a damp cloth and leave for about 10 minutes, then peel off the skin and chop the flesh roughly.

❷ Heat the milk, butter and flour together, stirring all the time, until thickened and boiling. Cook for 1 to 2 minutes, then season to taste and turn into a large bowl. Mix the aubergine with the spring onions and oregano, then add to the sauce. Add the almonds, more seasoning and breadcrumbs to give a thick paste. Shape into 8 rissoles, flouring your hands as necessary.

❸ Heat the oil in a large pan. Dip each rissole in the beaten egg and then in the toasted breadcrumbs, pressing on the crumbs. Add the rissoles to the pan and fry gently for 4 to 5 minutes on each side. Serve immediately with tartare sauce and salad.

97

Aubergine Olives with Nuts and Cheese

This makes a colourful vegetarian dish. If you are cooking it for friends and don't want any last-minute bother, it can be prepared well in advance and kept in the refrigerator until needed

SERVES 4

- 1 large aubergine, cut lengthways into 8 slices
- Salt and freshly ground black pepper
- Olive oil, for frying
- 1 large onion, roughly chopped
- 1 small handful of fresh parsley
- 100 g/3½ oz walnut pieces
- 100 g/3½ oz mushrooms, roughly chopped
- 75 g/2¾ oz wholewheat breadcrumbs
- Butter, for greasing
- 400 g/14 oz tinned chopped tomatoes
- 75 g/2¾ oz grated Cheddar cheese

Preparation and salting time: 1 hour

Cooking time: 40 minutes

---

❶ Arrange the aubergine slices in a single layer on a baking sheet, then sprinkle liberally with salt and leave to stand for at least 30 minutes. Rinse well under cold water, then pat dry on paper towels.

❷ Preheat the oven to 190°C/375°F/ Gas Mark 5. Heat 2 to 3 tablespoons of olive oil in a large pan. Add the aubergine slices and fry on both sides until just soft. Remove from the pan and lay on a plate.

❸ Place the onions, parsley, nuts and mushrooms in a food processor and process until chopped very fine. Heat 1 to 2 more tablespoons of oil in the pan, then add the onion mixture and fry gently for 2 to 3 minutes. Stir in the breadcrumbs and season well.

❹ Place a little of the nut mixture on each slice of aubergine, then roll up and secure with wooden cocktail sticks. Place in a buttered ovenproof dish, then season lightly. Pour the chopped tomatoes over the aubergine olives, then scatter the grated cheese over them.

❺ Bake in the preheated oven for 40 minutes, until the cheese is browned and the aubergine is tender.

Mixed Vegetable Gumbo

Gumbo is a traditional dish of okra and spices from the southern states of America. It usually contains chicken or fish, but make it with just a good selection of vegetables for vegetarian friends.

SERVES 4

- 100 ml/3½ fl oz olive oil
- 2 large onions, chopped
- 1 red and 1 green pepper, cored, seeded and cut into 1-cm/½-inch squares
- 1 hot chilli, seeded and finely sliced
- 2 garlic cloves, finely sliced
- 500 g/1 lb 2 oz okra, cut into 1-cm/ ½-inch slices
- 400 g/14 oz tinned chopped tomatoes
- 2 Tbsp butter
- 3 Tbsp flour
- 2 tsp chilli powder
- 1 tsp ground cumin
- 850 ml/1½ pt vegetable stock
- 4–5 sprigs fresh thyme
- Salt and freshly ground black pepper
- 1 aubergine, cut into 2-cm/1-inch pieces
- 1 long, thin aubergine, sliced
- Boiled rice, to serve (optional)

Preparation time: 40 minutes

Cooking time: 1 hour

❶ Heat 3 tablespoons of oil in a large pan. Add the onion and cook gently until softened but not browned. Add the peppers, chilli powder, garlic and okra. Cook for 5 minutes over a very low heat, then add the tomatoes. Cover and simmer for 15 minutes.

❷ Meanwhile, melt the butter in a large flameproof casserole, then add the flour and spices and cook over a low heat until bubbling gently. Remove from the heat and gradually add the stock, then the thyme. Return to the heat and bring slowly to the boil. Simmer the sauce for 1 to 2 minutes; it should be quite thin, even after boiling. Season well, then add the vegetable mixture. Cover and cook slowly for 30 minutes.

❸ Heat the remaining oil in a large pan, add the chopped aubergine and fry until browned. Transfer to the gumbo and simmer for a further 15 minutes.

❹ Add the aubergine slices to the pan and cook on both sides. Season, then serve garnished with the fried aubergine.

Aubergine with Garlic and Tomatoes

A quick and simple dish to cook when time is short.

SERVES 2

- 1 aubergine, sliced
- 1 large onion, sliced
- 1–2 tsp paprika
- 5 Tbsp olive oil
- 4 garlic cloves, peeled but left whole
- 8 halves of sun-dried tomatoes in oil, shredded finely
- 2 Tbsp oil from the tomatoes
- Salt and freshly ground black pepper
- 2–3 Tbsp chopped fresh parsley

Preparation time: 10 minutes

Cooking time: 20 minutes

❶ Toss the aubergine and onion in the paprika. Heat the oil in a large pan, add the aubergine and onion and cook for 3 to 4 minutes. Add the garlic and cook for 2 to 3 minutes, then add the tomatoes and their oil.

❷ Continue to stir-fry for 8 to 10 minutes, until the aubergine is tender, and the onion and garlic have caramelized slightly. Season, then add the parsley before serving.

Imam Bayaldi - *the Imam fainted*

Although I have found many differing recipes for this time-honoured dish, here's mine! The dish is served cold. The title comes from the legend that the Imam, or holy man, was overcome by the delicious aroma when this was cooked for him!

SERVES 4

- 4 large aubergines
- Salt
- 150 ml/5 fl oz fruity olive oil
- Juice of 1 lemon
- 1 tsp caster sugar
- About 600 ml/1 pt thick tomato juice
- Chopped fresh parsley, to garnish

STUFFING:

- 225 g/8 oz tomatoes, skinned and chopped
- 1 large onion, finely chopped
- 3 Tbsp chopped fresh parsley
- Salt and freshly ground black pepper
- 1 tsp ground cinnamon

Preparation and salting time:

1½ hours

Cooking time: 1 hour

Chilling time: 2 hours

❶ Score the eggplant flesh every 1 cm/½ inch. Pare away alternate strips of skin, to make stripes. Stand the aubergines in a colander, sprinkle with salt and leave for 30 to 60 minutes. Rinse well, then dry.

❷ Combine all the ingredients for the stuffing. Slit the aubergines on one side and pack the stuffing into them, then place in a covered sauté pan, slit side uppermost.

❸ Pour the oil and lemon juice over the aubergines and sprinkle with the sugar. Add just enough tomato juice to cover them. Cover the pan and simmer slowly for about 1 hour, until the aubergines are soft. Alternatively, bake them for about 1 hour at 160°C/325°F/Gas Mark 3.

❹ Season the sauce once the aubergines are cooked, then allow them to cool completely. Chill for about 1 hour, then serve with the tomato sauce spooned over, with a rice salad or lettuce leaves.

Imam Bayaldi

Spaghetti with Aubergine and Courgettes

A very simple recipe becomes something special with the addition of pine nuts and aubergine slices.

SERVES 4

- Olive oil, for frying
- 40 g/1½ oz pine nuts
- 1 large aubergine, sliced
- 450 g/1 lb spaghetti
- 2 large courgettes, sliced
- 1–2 garlic cloves, crushed
- 2 Tbsp torn basil leaves and chopped fresh parsley, mixed
- Salt and freshly ground black pepper
- Freshly grated Parmesan cheese, to serve

Preparation time: 10 minutes

Cooking time: 20 minutes

---

❶ Bring a large saucepan of salted water to the boil. Heat a little oil in a large pan, add the pine nuts and cook until golden. Remove with a slotted spoon and leave on a plate, then add the aubergine with more oil and fry until starting to soften and brown.

❷ Add the pasta to the boiling water, return to the boil and simmer until *al dente* (cooked, that is, until it offers a slight resistance when bitten, but is not soft or overdone).

❸ Add the courgettes and garlic to the pan and continue frying for 8 to 10 minutes until all the vegetables are soft and golden.

❹ Drain the pasta and add it to the pan with the herbs. Season to taste. Add the pine nuts and toss well. Serve immediately, with grated Parmesan.

TIP

Fresh pasta cooks in about 2 to 3 minutes, while good-quality dried pasta may take 10 to 12 minutes. You need lots of water and generous amounts of salt. Allow ½ teaspoon salt to 1.2 l/2 pints of boiling water.

---

vegetable dishes

Vegetable Loaf

A really tasty, vegetable loaf. Serve with a tomato or mushroom sauce, or a good spoonful of spicy fruit chutney.

SERVES 6

- 150 g/5½ oz brown rice
- 3–4 Tbsp olive oil
- 1 large aubergine, thickly sliced
- 1 large onion
- 2 courgettes
- 2 garlic cloves, crushed
- 150 g/51/2 oz wholewheat breadcrumbs
- 1 large egg, beaten
- 75 g/2¾ oz grated Cheddar cheese
- Salt and freshly ground black pepper
- Butter, for greasing

Preparation time: 1 hour

Cooking time: 40 minutes

❶ Cook the rice in a large pan of water until tender. Do not add salt as it will toughen the rice. Drain in a colander.

❷ Preheat the oven to 190ºC/375ºF/ Gas Mark 5. Heat 1 to 2 tablespoons of olive oil in a large pan, add the aubergine slices and fry until just tender. Remove, and allow to cool.

❸ Shred the onion and courgettes. Heat 2 tablespoons of olive oil in a pan, add the vegetables and cook until just tender. Turn into a large bowl and add the rice, garlic, breadcrumbs, egg and cheese.

Season to taste and mix thoroughly.

❹ Butter a large loaf pan, about 18 x 9 x 7 cm/7 x 3½ x 2½ inches, and line the bottom with baking parchment. Arrange half the aubergine slices in a layer in the bottom of the pan, then top with half the rice mixture. Make a second layer of aubergine in the middle of

the loaf and top with the remaining rice, packing it down firmly. Cover with buttered foil.

❺ Bake the loaf in the preheated oven for 40 minutes. Remove the foil and ease the loaf away from the tin with a knife. Turn the loaf onto a warmed serving plate and serve sliced.

Aubergines Stuffed with Mushroom and Egg

These stuffed aubergines have a very fresh and delicate flavour. You could serve them with a parsley sauce if you like, although it is a good, low-fat dish on its own.

SERVES 4

- 2 large aubergines
- 2 Tbsp olive oil
- 1 large onion, chopped
- 125 g/4½ oz mushrooms, roughly chopped
- 350 ml/12 fl oz well-flavoured stock
- 2 Tbsp tomato paste
- 2 hard-boiled eggs, roughly chopped
- 1 Tbsp chopped fresh flat-leaf parsley
- Salt and freshly ground black pepper

Preparation time: 40 minutes

Cooking time: 30 minutes

---

❶ Cut the aubergines in half lengthways, leaving on the stalks to help keep them in shape when they are baking. Carefully scrape out the flesh, leaving a shell about 6 mm/ ¼ inch thick. Salt the shells lightly and leave them upside down on paper towels to drain while preparing the filling. Roughly chop the aubergine flesh.

❷ Preheat the oven to 200°C/400°F/ Gas Mark 6. Heat the oil in a pan. Add the onion and cook until softened but not browned, then add the mushrooms and cook for a further minute. Stir the aubergine flesh into the pan, then add the stock and tomato paste. Bring to the boil, then simmer quite quickly, uncovered, for about 20 minutes.

❸ Rinse the aubergine shells in cold water, then drain well and place in an ovenproof dish. When the aubergine is cooked and the mixture has become a thick sauce, add the chopped eggs and parsley to the sauce, then season to taste.

❹ Divide the filling between the aubergines, then pour a little boiling water into the bottom of the dish. Cover the dish with foil, then bake for 30 minutes, until the aubergine shells are tender. Serve immediately with freshly cooked green vegetables such as broccoli, courgettes or peas.

Aubergine and Sweet Potato Curry

This makes a very substantial main course, but it could also be served as a side dish with meat or fish curries.

S ERVES 4

- 2 tsp cumin seeds
- 1 Tbsp mustard seeds
- 3 Tbsp ghee or sunflower oil
- 2 small sweet potatoes, about 500 g/ 1 lb 2 oz, peeled and cut into 1-cm/ ½-inch chunks
- 1 large onion, finely sliced
- 2 garlic cloves, finely sliced
- 1–2 tsp chilli powder
- 1 tsp ground turmeric
- 1 large aubergine, cut the same size as the potato
- 1 Tbsp poppy seeds
- 250 ml/9 fl oz water or vegetable stock
- 2 tsp salt
- 1 Tbsp torn fresh coriander leaves

Preparation time: 15 minutes

Cooking time: 45 minutes

❶ Heat a large pan over a medium heat, then add the cumin and mustard seeds and fry for 30 seconds or so, until aromatic and starting to pop. Transfer to a plate and leave to cool.

❷ Heat the ghee or oil in the pan, add the potatoes and cook for 3 to 4 minutes until starting to soften. Add the onion, garlic, chilli powder and turmeric and cook for 1 to 2 minutes, then add the aubergine with the roasted spices and the poppy seeds. Stir in the water and salt, then cover and simmer very slowly for 30 to 45 minutes, until the vegetables are tender.

❸ Season the curry to taste, then serve sprinkled with the torn coriander leaves.

Lentil Moussaka

A meatless variation of the classic baked dish. This is rich, filling and full of fibre, so it must be good for you!

SERVES 4 TO 6

- Olive oil, for frying
- 1 large onion, chopped
- 2 garlic cloves, crushed
- 1 green pepper, cored, seeded and chopped
- 2 Tbsp olive oil
- 175 g/6 oz red lentils
- About 150 ml/5 fl oz red wine
- 400 g/14 oz tinned chopped tomatoes
- Salt and freshly ground black pepper
- 1 Tbsp chopped fresh oregano
- 2 large aubergines, sliced
- 600 ml/1 pt milk
- 4 Tbsp butter, plus extra for greasing
- 4 Tbsp plain flour
- 75 g/2¾ oz grated Cheddar cheese

Preparation time: 45 minutes
Cooking time: 30 minutes

---

❶ Preheat the oven to 220°C/425°F/ Gas Mark 7. Heat 2 tablespoons of oil in a large pan. Add the onion, garlic and pepper and cook gently until soft. Add the lentils, red wine and tomatoes. Bring to the boil, then season and add the oregano. Simmer for 20 minutes, or until the lentils are soft. Add a little more wine or stock to the sauce if it seems dry.

❷ Meanwhile, heat 2 to 3 tablespoons of oil in a large pan. Fry the aubergine slices on both sides until tender, adding more oil if necessary, then drain on paper towels. Add any oil left in the pan to the lentil sauce.

❸ Heat the milk, butter and flour together in a pan, stirring all the time, until boiling and thickened. Continue to cook for 1 minute, to remove the taste of flour from the sauce, then remove the pan from the heat. Add all but 2 tablespoons of the grated cheese. Season to taste.

❹ Layer the lentil sauce and aubergine slices in a buttered, ovenproof dish, finishing with a layer of aubergine. Spoon the cheese sauce over the aubergine, then scatter the remaining cheese over the top. Bake in the preheated oven for 30 minutes, until the moussaka is browned and set. Serve immediately.

vegetable dishes

Nut and Aubergine Sausages

The nuts give a good texture to these sausages. Do cook them slowly, or the nuts will burn and stick.

SERVES 4

- 1 aubergine
- 125 g/4½ oz instant potato granules
- 450 ml/16 fl oz boiling water
- Salt and freshly ground black pepper
- 6 spring onions, very finely chopped
- 2 Tbsp chopped fresh oregano or parsley
- 125 g/4½ oz mixed chopped nuts
- Flour, if necessary
- 3–4 Tbsp olive oil

Preparation time: 1 hour

Cooking time: 10 minutes

---

❶ Cook the aubergine over a barbecue, under the grill or in a hot oven until the skin is wrinkled and blistered, and the flesh is tender, turning from time to time. Cover with a damp cloth, then leave for 10 minutes until cool enough to handle. Peel off the skin.

❷ Mix the potato with the boiling water and add salt and pepper. Purée the aubergine in a food processor, then add it to the potato with the spring onions, herbs and nuts. Shape the mixture into 8 thick sausages.

❸ Heat 2 to 3 tablespoons of olive oil in a large pan, then fry the sausages gently until lightly browned on all sides. Serve with a blue cheese dressing or fruity chutney.

Aubergine and Tomato Gratin

The potatoes in this gratin turn it into a substantial supper dish.

SERVES 4

- Olive oil, for frying
- 2 large aubergines, thickly sliced
- 1 large onion, chopped
- 500 g/1 lb 2 oz potatoes, thickly sliced
- 2 garlic cloves, finely sliced
- Salt and freshly ground black pepper
- 8 ripe tomatoes, sliced
- 150 ml/5 fl oz well-flavoured stock
- 75 g/2¾ oz mixed grated cheeses: Cheddar, blue cheese, mozzarella
- 50 g/1¾ oz fresh breadcrumbs

Preparation time: 15 minutes

Cooking time: 40 minutes

---

❶ Heat 2 to 3 tablespoons of the oil in a large pan, add the aubergine slices and fry until lightly browned on both sides. Remove them with a slotted spoon. Add the onion and sliced potatoes to the pan, with a little extra oil if necessary, and cook until starting to soften. Stir in the garlic and season to taste. Return the aubergines to the pan with the sliced tomatoes, add the stock, then cover the pan and cook slowly for 30 minutes, or until all the vegetables are tender. Season.

❷ Turn the vegetables into a buttered, ovenproof gratin dish, with as much of the cooking liquor as you wish. Mix the cheeses with the bread crumbs and scatter over the vegetables. Grill until the cheese has melted and browned. Serve immediately.

Aubergine and Tomato Gratin

109

Aubergine and Tomato Galette

I like to serve this as a supper dish, but it could easily be stretched to feed more as an appetizer. Although it takes some time to prepare, the work can all be done in advance so that the galette can be baked at the last moment.

SERVES 4

- Butter, for greasing
- 6 large eggs, beaten
- 50 ml/1¾ fl oz milk
- Salt and freshly ground black pepper
- 1 large aubergine, sliced
- Olive oil, for frying
- 4 tomatoes, sliced
- 1–2 garlic cloves, thinly sliced
- 125 g/4½ oz mozzarella, thinly sliced

SAUCE:

- 150 ml/5 fl oz soured cream
- 150 ml/5 fl oz thick natural yogurt
- 2 Tbsp chopped chives
- Grated zest and juice of ½ lemon

Preparation time: 45 minutes

Cooking time: 25 minutes

---

❶ Preheat the oven to 200°C/400°F/ Gas Mark 6, and butter a round gratin dish, the same diameter as your omelette pan. Beat the eggs with the milk and a little seasoning, then use to make 3 fairly thick omelettes. Stack the finished omelettes on paper towels until required. (I finish the top of each omelette under a hot grill, to save turning them over in the pan.)

❷ Heat 2 to 3 tablespoons of olive oil in a pan. Add the aubergine and cook until just tender and lightly browned, adding more oil as necessary. Place one omelette in the bottom of the buttered dish, then arrange half the aubergine slices in a layer on top. Season lightly, then cover with half the sliced tomatoes and garlic. Season again and top with a third of the mozzarella. Repeat the layers, finishing with an omelette topped with mozzarella.

❸ Bake in the preheated oven for 20 to 25 minutes, until the galette is piping hot and the mozzarella has melted and is lightly browned.

❹ Mix all the ingredients for the sauce together while the galette is baking. Serve the galette cut into quarters, with the sauce spooned over and around it.

Aubergine and Tomato Gratin

Aubergine and Tomato Galette

I like to serve this as a supper dish, but it could easily be stretched to feed more as an appetizer. Although it takes some time to prepare, the work can all be done in advance so that the galette can be baked at the last moment.

SERVES 4

- Butter, for greasing
- 6 large eggs, beaten
- 50 ml/1¾ fl oz milk
- Salt and freshly ground black pepper
- 1 large aubergine, sliced
- Olive oil, for frying
- 4 tomatoes, sliced
- 1–2 garlic cloves, thinly sliced
- 125 g/4½ oz mozzarella, thinly sliced

SAUCE:

- 150 ml/5 fl oz soured cream
- 150 ml/5 fl oz thick natural yogurt
- 2 Tbsp chopped chives
- Grated zest and juice of ½ lemon

Preparation time: 45 minutes

Cooking time: 25 minutes

---

❶ Preheat the oven to 200°C/400°F/ Gas Mark 6, and butter a round gratin dish, the same diameter as your omelette pan. Beat the eggs with the milk and a little seasoning, then use to make 3 fairly thick omelettes. Stack the finished omelettes on paper towels until required. (I finish the top of each omelette under a hot grill, to save turning them over in the pan.)

❷ Heat 2 to 3 tablespoons of olive oil in a pan. Add the aubergine and cook until just tender and lightly browned, adding more oil as necessary. Place one omelette in the bottom of the buttered dish, then arrange half the aubergine slices in a layer on top. Season lightly, then cover with half the sliced tomatoes and garlic. Season again and top with a third of the mozzarella. Repeat the layers, finishing with an omelette topped with mozzarella.

❸ Bake in the preheated oven for 20 to 25 minutes, until the galette is piping hot and the mozzarella has melted and is lightly browned.

❹ Mix all the ingredients for the sauce together while the galette is baking. Serve the galette cut into quarters, with the sauce spooned over and around it.

vegetable dishes

Aubergine and Wild Rice Bake

I love casseroles of wild rice, so for this recipe I decided to make a thick casserole which would give a fragrant, moist filling between layers of aubergine.

SERVES 4

- About 6 Tbsp olive oil
- 1 large onion, finely chopped
- 1–2 garlic cloves, crushed
- 1 large carrot, finely chopped
- 1 green pepper, cored, seeded and chopped
- 175 g/6 oz wild rice
- 400 g/14 oz tinned chopped tomatoes
- 250 ml/9 fl oz well-flavoured stock
- 2 large aubergines, thickly sliced
- 1 Tbsp chopped fresh oregano
- Salt and freshly ground black pepper
- 100 g/3½ oz soft goat's cheese, crumbled (optional)

Preparation time: 1 hour

Cooking time: 20 minutes

❶ Heat 2 tablespoons of oil in a pan. Add the onion and garlic and cook until softened but not browned, then add the carrot and cook for a further 2 minutes or so. Stir in the pepper and rice, then add the chopped tomatoes and stock. Bring to the boil, then cover the pan and simmer for 50 to 60 minutes, or until the rice is tender.

❷ Meanwhile, heat 3 to 4 tablespoons of olive oil in a pan. Add the aubergine slices and cook lightly on both sides. Add more oil as necessary, but try not to use too much as this is otherwise a fairly low-fat recipe. Preheat the oven to 190°C/375°F/Gas Mark 5.

❸ Layer half the aubergine slices in the bottom of an ovenproof dish. Add the chopped oregano to the rice, then season to taste. Pour the rice over the aubergine, then top with the remaining slices. Season lightly and crumble the goat's cheese over the top, if using. Bake in the preheated oven for 20 minutes. Serve with a green salad.

TIP

Wild rice, harvested only in America, and in fact a type of grass seed, has a nutty flavour. It gives a luxurious touch to create a special meal.

vegetable dishes

111

Tortillas Stuffed with Aubergine and Chilli

Flour tortillas are easy to use and can turn almost any combination of ingredients into a quick Tex Mex meal. You could used chopped spring onions or avocado as additional salad garnishes. Leave the chilli unseeded if you like your tortillas hot.

SERVES 4

- 1 large aubergine, cut into 1-cm/½-inch chunks
- 1 onion, finely chopped
- 1 tsp chilli powder
- 5 Tbsp groundnut oil
- 1 green chilli, seeded and chopped
- 1 garlic clove, finely chopped
- 50 g/1¾ oz pecan nuts, roughly chopped
- 8 flour tortillas

TO SERVE:

- Grated Cheddar cheese
- Shredded lettuce
- Chopped tomatoes
- Soured cream

Preparation time: 10 minutes

Cooking time: 15 minutes

---

❶ Toss the aubergine and onion in the chilli powder. Heat the oil in a large pan, add the aubergine and onion, and fry gently until lightly browned on all sides, about 5 minutes. Add the chilli, garlic and pecans and continue cooking for a further 5 minutes, or until all the vegetables are tender.

❷ Meanwhile, heat the flour tortillas, either in the oven or in a microwave according to the instructions on the packet.

❸ To serve, place some of the aubergine mixture in the centre of each tortilla, then top with a little cheese, lettuce, soured cream and tomatoes. Fold the bottom of the tortilla upwards, then roll the sides over to enclose the filling.

Chickpea and Aubergine Stew

A rich vegetable stew with a sesame-flavoured sauce and a crisp salsa garnish.
I suggest serving this with garlic bread and a green leaf salad.

SERVES 4

- 175 g/6 oz chickpeas, soaked overnight
- 50 ml/2 fl oz olive oil
- 1 large onion, finely sliced
- 2 aubergines, sliced
- Grated zest and juice of 1 lemon
- 1–2 garlic cloves, finely sliced
- 250 ml/9 fl oz dry white wine
- 450 ml/16 fl oz stock
- Salt and freshly ground black pepper
- 2 bay leaves
- 4 Tbsp chopped fresh mixed herbs, such as flat-leaf parsley, marjoram, oregano, tarragon etc.
- 4 Tbsp tahini paste

SALSA:

- 1 orange
- 2 tomatoes, chopped
- ½ cucumber, chopped
- 1 red onion, finely chopped
- 1 Tbsp chopped fresh parsley

Preparation time: 20 minutes
plus overnight soaking
Cooking time: 1½ hours

---

❶ Drain the chickpeas and rinse them thoroughly. Place in a large pan with enough water to cover and bring to the boil. Boil rapidly for 10 minutes, then reduce the heat and leave to simmer slowly.

❷ Meanwhile, heat the oil in a pan. Add the onion and aubergine and cook until softened and just starting to brown; do not add any extra oil as this dish will be quite rich. Drain the chickpeas and add to the pan with the grated lemon zest, garlic, wine and stock. Stir well, add the seasonings, then bring to the boil. Cover and simmer slowly for 1 hour, or until the chickpeas are tender.

❸ While the chickpeas are cooking, prepare the salsa. Pare the zest from the orange and place it in a bowl. Peel the fruit, then chop the flesh into small dice. Add all the remaining salsa ingredients. Season to taste, then allow to stand.

❹ Stir the tahini into the chickpea mixture, then season well. Serve in deep plates, with a good spoonful of salsa on each helping.

Aubergine and Fennel Relish

Sweet Aubergine and Mango Chutney

Aubergines Preserved with Mint

Aubergine Salsa with Tomatoes

Aubergine and Mint Relish

Aubergine-stuffed Parathas

Indian-Style Aubergine Relish

Mustard Seed and Aubergine Salsa

Warm Aubergine and Courgette Salsa

Aubergine and Walnut Bread

Aubergine and Nutmeg Ice Cream

Aubergine and Fennel Relish

I have added some fresh fennel to the aubergine in this Arabic-style relish, which provides a little contrast in texture. Fennel and aubergine have very complementary flavours. This is a relish which looks well in a preserving jar.

MAKES ABOUT 2 KG/4½ LB

- 1 kg/2 lb 4 oz small young aubergines, halved and cut into 5-cm/2-inch chunks
- Salt
- 2 Tbsp coriander seeds
- 2 Tbsp fennel seeds
- About 350 ml/12½ fl oz fruity olive oil
- 1 fennel bulb, finely sliced
- Fine sea salt
- 2 Tbsp black peppercorns
- 100 ml/3½ fl oz red wine vinegar

Preparation time: 1 hour for salting

Cooking time: 15 minutes

---

❶ Layer the aubergines in a colander with salt and leave for at least 1 hour. Rinse thoroughly under cold running water, then pat dry on paper towels.

❷ Heat a large pan over a moderate heat, then add the coriander and fennel seeds and fry them for about 30 seconds, until fragrant and starting to brown. Transfer to a plate and leave to cool.

❸ Heat 100 ml/3½ fl oz of olive oil in the pan, then add the aubergine and fennel and cook for about 5 minutes, until the aubergine is lightly browned. Remove with a slotted spoon and allow to drain on paper towels.

❹ Pack the aubergine and fennel into warmed preserving jars, seasoning the layers lightly with salt and packing the vegetables pieces down firmly with the back of a spoon. Scatter each layer with the toasted seeds mixed with peppercorns.

❺ Mix any oil remaining in the pan with the vinegar and sufficient olive oil to cover the vegetables: the mixture should be about one part vinegar to two parts oil. Seal the jars, then leave in a cool, dark place for about a week before serving. Eat within 4 to 6 weeks. Always store in the refrigerator.

relishes and accompaniments

Sweet Aubergine and Mango Chutney

This is a sweet but hot chutney, ideal for serving with curries, or with bread and cheese at a picnic lunch.

MAKES ABOUT 4 x 450 G/1 LB JARS

- 4 small green mangoes, ripe but firm, peeled and cut into chunks
- 2 aubergines, cut into 2-cm/1-inch chunks
- 2–3 garlic cloves, crushed
- 2 hot red chillies, finely chopped
- 75 g/2¾ oz finely chopped fresh ginger
- 1 Tbsp chilli powder
- 1 Tbsp coarse sea salt
- 600 ml/1 pt malt vinegar
- 900 g/2 lb demerara sugar

Preparation time: 10 minutes
plus 1 hour for salting
Cooking time: 1 hour

---

❶ Layer the mangoes and aubergines in a colander, salting them lightly. Leave for 1 hour, then rinse well in cold water and drain.

❷ Place the mangoes and aubergines in a large pan with all the remaining ingredients. Bring slowly to the boil, then cook gently for 45 to 60 minutes, until the chutney is well reduced but still juicily moist.

❸ Pour into warmed jars, packing the mixture well down, then seal and label. Leave for 3 to 4 weeks to mature before eating.

relishes and accompaniments

117

Aubergines Preserved with Mint

Try to use preserving jars for this recipe, as they make excellent presents. The aubergines must remain completely covered by the oil to be properly preserved.

MAKES ABOUT 2 KG/4¼ LB

- 1 kg/2 lb 4 oz small aubergines
- Salt
- 600 ml/1 pt white wine vinegar
- 6–8 garlic cloves, according to size, finely sliced
- 1 large handful fresh mint leaves, left whole
- 1 Tbsp mixed peppercorns
- 2 large green chillies, seeded and finely shredded
- 450 ml/16 fl oz fruity olive oil

Preparation time: 2–3 hours or overnight for salting

Cooking time: 15 minutes

❶ Cut the aubergines into quarters lengthways, then into 5-cm/2-inch chunks. Layer them in a colander with plenty of salt. Leave to stand for 2 to 3 hours, or overnight. Rinse thoroughly, then drain and shake dry.

❷ Bring the vinegar to the boil in a deep pan, then add the aubergines and garlic and boil for 5 minutes. Stir once or twice, to keep the aubergines covered with the vinegar. Drain and allow to cool completely.

❸ Layer the aubergines and garlic alternately with the mint in warm, clean preserving jars. Season each layer with a mixture of the peppercorns and sliced chillies, and pack the layers tightly by pressing down firmly with a wooden spoon.

❹ Pour half the oil into the jars, to just cover the aubergines, then cover and leave overnight. By the next day, the aubergines will have absorbed much of the oil. Add sufficient extra oil to cover the aubergines completely, then seal the jar and leave for at least a week before serving.

relishes and accompaniments

118

Aubergine Salsa with Tomatoes

Most salsas are made with raw vegetables and fruits, so this is an unusual combination of half cooked and half raw vegetables. Use a yellow pepper for colour if yellow tomatoes are not available.

SERVES 4

- 4 Tbsp fruity olive oil
- 1 large aubergine, cut into 6-mm/ ¼-inch dice
- 1 red onion, finely chopped
- 4 red tomatoes, seeded and chopped
- 2 yellow tomatoes, seeded and chopped
- 1 green chilli, seeded and finely chopped
- 1 avocado, peeled and cut into 1-cm/½-inch chunks
- Grated zest and juice of 1 lime
- Salt and freshly ground black pepper
- 3 Tbsp freshly chopped coriander

Preparation time: 10 minutes
Cooking time: 10 minutes
---

❶ Heat the oil in a pan. Add the aubergine and cook until browned and tender, then remove with a slotted spoon and place in a salad bowl. Allow the aubergine to cool. Reserve any oil left in the pan.

❷ Add all the remaining ingredients to the bowl, tossing the avocado in the lime juice. Season well, then finally stir in any remaining oil and the coriander leaves. Allow to stand before serving, to allow the flavours to blend.

Aubergine and Mint Relish

This is almost a vegetable sauce, but the ingredients are chunky. It is excellent with kebabs or lentil patties. Remove the chilli seeds for a cooler relish.

SERVES 4 TO 6

- 4 Tbsp fruity olive oil
- 1 large onion, finely chopped
- 1 aubergine, cut into 1-cm/½-inch dice
- 2 garlic cloves, finely chopped
- 2 large green peppers, cored, seeded and cut into 6-mm/¼-inch dice
- 1 red chilli, finely sliced
- 1 Tbsp white wine vinegar
- Salt and freshly ground black pepper
- Sugar, to taste

Preparation time: 10 minutes
Cooking time: 10 minutes
---

❶ Heat the oil in a pan, add the onion and aubergine and cook until tender and lightly browned. Add the garlic and peppers, and continue cooking for a further 2 minutes, until the peppers are slightly softened.

❷ Remove the pan from the heat and stir in the chilli – it has more impact if added raw. Turn the relish into a serving dish, then add the vinegar and season to taste, adding a little sugar if necessary. Serve the relish warm or cold.

Aubergine-stuffed Parathas

These flatbreads are almost a meal in themselves. Serve with any spiced dish, or as a tasty snack in their own right.

MAKES 6

- 450 g/1 lb wholewheat flour, plus extra for dusting
- ½ tsp salt
- About 300 ml/10 fl oz water
- Vegetable oil or melted ghee, for frying
- 1–2 Tbsp butter
- Yogurt or relish, to serve

FILLING:

- 3 Tbsp vegetable or groundnut oil
- 1 aubergine, cut into 6-mm/¼-inch dice
- ½ tsp chilli powder
- ½ tsp ground turmeric
- 1 Tbsp finely chopped fresh ginger
- 2 green chillies, seeded and finely chopped
- 2 Tbsp chopped fresh coriander
- 1 tsp salt

Preparation time: 30 minutes

Cooking time: 15 minutes

---

❶ First make the filling. Heat the oil in a pan. Add the aubergine with the chilli powder and turmeric and cook until soft, then add the remaining ingredients for the filling and mix well. Remove from the heat and leave to cool.

❷ Mix the flour and salt to a firm, manageable dough with cold water, then knead until pliable. Cover with a bowl and leave for 10 minutes.

❸ Divide the dough into 6 pieces. Work with one piece of dough at a time, leaving the others covered until required. Roll out to a circle about 10 cm/4 inches in diameter, then place some filling on the dough. Fold the edges over to enclose the filling, then dip the dough in a little extra flour and roll it out into a circle about 17 cm/7 inches in diameter. The aubergine may break through the dough; try not to press too hard on the edges of the dough when rolling. If necessary, sprinkle a little extra flour over the dough to hold the filling.

❹ Heat a griddle or large frying pan over a moderate heat, then cook the parathas briefly for about 1 minute on each side. Brush each side with melted ghee or oil and cook gently until lightly browned and crisp. Keep the parathas warm wrapped in a clean cloth in a very low oven until they are all cooked. Serve hot, dotted with butter and with a spoonful of yogurt or relish.

Indian-style Aubergine Relish

Most Indian relishes contain a large quantity of oil and are very hot, and this is no exception. It is an excellent relish to add in small quantities to prawn curries.

MAKES ABOUT 2 KG/2¼ LB

- 500 g/1 lb 2 oz firm young aubergines, cut into 2-cm/1-inch chunks
- Salt
- 1 Tbsp cumin seeds
- 300 ml/10 fl oz groundnut oil
- 2 large onions, chopped
- 4 garlic cloves, finely chopped
- 5-cm/2-inch piece fresh ginger, peeled and finely chopped
- 1 tsp ground turmeric
- 2 Tbsp demerara sugar
- 4 hot red chillies, finely sliced
- 2 green chillies, finely sliced

Preparation time: 10 minutes

plus 1 hour for salting

Cooking time: 10 minutes

---

❶ Layer the aubergines in a colander with salt and leave for at least 1 hour. Rinse thoroughly under cold running water, then pat dry on paper towels.

❷ Heat a large pan over moderate heat, then add the cumin seeds and fry them for 30 seconds, until fragrant and just starting to colour. Tip onto a plate and leave to cool.

❸ Heat the oil in the pan. Add the aubergines and onion and cook for 3 to 4 minutes, then add the garlic, ginger and turmeric and continue cooking for a further 2 minutes. Allow to cool slightly, then mix the sugar into the oil with 1 teaspoon of salt.

❹ Pack the aubergines and onions into warmed jars, layering them with the sliced chillies. Press down firmly on each layer with the back of a spoon to exclude all air from the jars. Pour as much of the oil into the jars as possible, then seal.

❺ Keep the relish for at least 2 to 3 weeks before using; a month or so is better still. Store in the refrigerator to keep them cold, and use quickly once opened.

Mustard Seed and Aubergine Salsa

Roasting some spices to add to a salsa not only gives extra flavour, but texture too. The combination of aubergine, mustard seeds and orange here is especially good.

SERVES 4

- 1 Tbsp white mustard seeds
- 4 Tbsp olive oil
- 1 aubergine, cut into 6-mm/¼-inch dice
- 1 large orange
- 2 tomatoes, seeded and chopped
- 4 spring onions, finely chopped
- ½ cucumber, cut into 6-mm/¼-inch dice
- 2 rings of pineapple, cut into chunks
- Salt and freshly ground black pepper
- 2 Tbsp chopped fresh parsley

Preparation time: 10 minutes

Cooking time: 15 minutes

❶ Heat a large pan over a medium heat, then add the mustard seeds and fry for about 30 seconds, until they are just fragrant. Turn into a salad bowl.

❷ Heat the oil in the pan, add the aubergine and cook until lightly browned and tender. Transfer the aubergine to the salad bowl with a slotted spoon and leave until cold.

❸ Pare the zest from the orange and add it to the bowl, then peel and chop the fruit. Add the orange to the aubergine with the remaining ingredients and season. Add the parsley to the bowl, then allow to stand for 30 minutes before serving.

Warm Aubergine and Courgette Salsa

This is really a warm salad, so serve immediately. If kept warm, the vegetables will stew and the texture will be ruined.

SERVES 4

- 3 Tbsp pine nuts
- About 4 Tbsp olive oil
- 1 large aubergine, diced
- 2 courgettes, diced
- 4 tomatoes, seeded and diced
- 1 large yellow pepper, cored, seeded and cut into 6-mm/¼-inch dice
- 2 garlic cloves, finely shredded
- 12 basil leaves, finely shredded
- A few drops of balsamic vinegar
- Salt and freshly ground black pepper

Preparation time: 10 minutes

Cooking time: 10 minutes

❶ Heat a large pan over a medium heat. Add the pine nuts and fry for about 1 minute, tossing until they are golden brown. Remove from the pan and keep to one side on a plate.

❷ Heat 4 tablespoons of oil in the pan. Add the aubergine and cook for 2 minutes, then add the courgettes and continue cooking until the vegetables are tender, adding more oil if necessary.

❸ Stir the remaining ingredients into the pan and add the pine nuts. Season to taste and serve immediately.

Aubergine and Walnut Bread

The perfect picnic loaf to serve with a tomato and feta cheese salad. The loaf is much better made with fresh yeast if at all possible.

MAKES 1 LARGE LOAF

- 15 g/½ oz fresh yeast or 1 Tbsp dried fast-acting yeast
- 350 ml/12 fl oz tepid water
- 500 g/1 lb 2 oz strong white flour
- 125 g/4½ oz wholewheat flour
- 1 Tbsp salt
- 2 Tbsp walnut oil
- 40 g/1½ oz roughly chopped walnuts

FILLING:

- 1 large aubergine, finely sliced
- 1 onion, finely sliced
- 3–4 Tbsp walnut oil
- 1 tsp ground cinnamon
- 3 Tbsp seedless raisins
- Salt and freshly ground black pepper

Preparation time: 3 hours
Cooking time: 35 minutes

---

❶ Crumble the fresh yeast into the warm water and leave for 3 to 4 minutes, then stir until dissolved. If using dried yeast, mix with the flour. Mix the flours and salt together in a large bowl, then add the yeast liquid, or water if using dried yeast, and mix to a dough. Turn out onto a floured surface and knead for 10 minutes, until the dough is elastic in texture. Return the dough to the bowl, cover and leave in a warm place for about 1 hour, or until doubled in size.

❷ Meanwhile, prepare the filling. Heat the walnut oil in a pan, add the aubergine and onion and cook with the cinnamon until browned. Stir in the raisins, then season and allow to cool completely.

❸ Knock back the dough and reshape it, then return it to the bowl and leave covered for a further 30 minutes in a warm place.

❹ Lightly flour a baking sheet. Knock the dough back again, then knead in the chopped walnuts and divide the dough into 3 pieces. Roll the dough into 3 circles about 20 cm/8 inches in diameter. Place one circle on the floured baking sheet, top with half the filling then repeat the layers again, finishing with the last piece of dough. Seal the edges of the dough together with a little water, then cover with a damp cloth and leave in a warm place for 45 minutes to rise again. Preheat the oven to 240°C/475°F/Gas Mark 9.

❺ Bake the bread on the baking sheet in the preheated oven for 30 to 35 minutes, until browned and well risen. Remove from the oven and leave to cool on a wire rack. Serve with a tomato and feta cheese salad.

Aubergine and Nutmeg Ice Cream

Probably my most unusual ice-cream to date! Try it—it really is delicious.

Serves 4 to 6

- 1 small aubergine, sliced
- Caster or granulated sugar, for sprinkling

Vanilla syrup:

- 225 g/8 oz granulated sugar
- 1 vanilla pod
- 250 ml/9 fl oz water
- 4 green cardamoms, lightly crushed

Ice Cream:

- 300 ml/10 fl oz milk
- 1 vanilla pod
- 4 large egg yolks
- 75 g/2¾ oz caster sugar
- Freshly grated nutmeg, to taste—
  I use about half a nutmeg
- 300 ml/10 fl oz whipping cream

Preparation time: 10–12 hours
for the aubergine plus 2–3 hours
for ice cream
Freezing time: 25 minutes
in an ice-cream machine or
4–5 hours in a freezer

---

❶ Arrange the aubergine slices in a single layer on a baking sheet and sprinkle generously with sugar. Leave for 1 hour, so that any bitter juices are extracted.

❷ Prepare the vanilla syrup. Place the ingredients in a small pan and bring gently to the boil, stirring all the time until the sugar is dissolved. Boil for 10 to 15 minutes, until the syrup is well reduced. Meanwhile, rinse the aubergine slices thoroughly, then drain and dry on paper towels. Place the slices in the hot syrup. Remove the pan from the heat, cover and leave for 1 to 2 hours.

❸ Bring the aubergine slices to the boil in the syrup and simmer for 5 minutes. Leave to cool in the covered pan, then allow to stand for at least 8 hours, or overnight.

❹ Heat the milk with the second vanilla bean until almost at the boil, then cover and leave to stand, off the heat, for at least 20 minutes. Remove the vanilla bean and rinse well—it can be used again to flavour sugar. Beat the egg yolks with the sugar in a bowl until thick and pale. Reheat the milk until almost boiling, then pour it onto the eggs, whisking all the time, then add the nutmeg to taste. Rinse the milk pan in cold water, then return the custard to it and heat gently, until the mixture is just thick enough to coat the back of a wooden spoon. Turn the custard into a clean bowl and leave to cool completely. Chill for at least an hour before completing the ice cream.

❺ Fold the cream into the custard, then turn into an ice cream maker and freeze-churn until thick. Alternatively, freeze in a suitable plastic container for 4 to 5 hours, stirring the ice cream once or twice. Whip the cream before adding it to the custard if you do not use an ice-cream machine.

❻ Drain the aubergine slices to remove as much syrup as possible, then chop them very finely. Stir the aubergine into the ice cream just before it is ready.

❼ Freshly churned ice cream will need to harden in the freezer for 20 minutes before serving. Frozen ice cream must be tempered before it is suitable for serving. Allow about 20 minutes at normal room temperature.

Index

ACKNOWLEDGEMENTS

The publishers would like to thank West Dean Gardens of Chichester, Sussex, for opening their greenhouses for the photography featured on pages 6 through 14.